GREAT MEN SERIES

"The history of the world is but the biography of great men." So says Thomas Carlyle, and in the Great Men series we see history through the eyes of the men that shaped it.

Focusing on men of action, Imperium Press brings you biographies of the most consequential people who ever lived. History is best studied through the lives of great individuals, and the biographical form can teach like no other. In a world where decisive human will is needed more than ever, this series is sure to inspire and embolden.

GREAT MEN:
OLIVER CROMWELL

FREDERIC HARRISON

PERTH
IMPERIUM PRESS
2024

Published by Imperium Press

www.imperiumpress.org

Oliver Cromwell
published by Macmillan and Co. 1888

FIRST EDITION

NATIONAL LIBRARY OF AUSTRALIA

A catalogue record for this book is available from the National Library of Australia

ISBN 978-1-923104-40-2 Paperback
ISBN 978-1-923104-41-9 Hardcover
ISBN 978-1-923104-42-6 E-book

CONTENTS

OLIVER CROMWELL

CHAPTER I

BIRTH – PARENTAGE – EDUCATION

A.D. 1599–1620. AETAT. 1–21

Oliver Cromwell was horn at Huntingdon, on the 25th of April 1599. It was the dark year in Elizabeth's decline, which saw the fall of Essex and Tyrone's war. In the year preceding, Burleigh and Philip of Spain had both passed away; in the year following was born Charles the First. The sixteenth century, which had opened with such hopes, was closing in strife and gloom; the Tudor dynasty was in its wane; and the brilliant life of the Renascence had already deepened into the long struggle for conscience and freedom.

Oliver was the only surviving son of Robert Cromwell, the second son of Sir Henry Cromwell and younger brother of Sir Oliver Cromwell, both knights of Hinchinbrook, near Huntingdon. His mother was Elizabeth, the daughter of William Steward and sister of Sir Thomas Steward, both landowners of Ely. He came of a race well born and of good estate: as did Pym, Eliot, Hampden, Vane, St. John, Hutchinson, and Blake. "I was by birth a gentleman,"—so he told his first Parliament—"living neither in any considerable height, nor yet in obscurity." "Est Oliverius Cromwellus" wrote Milton, "genere nobili atque illustri ortus." The genealogists of later times have discovered for him traces of historic descent, which are more or less inventions, and were wholly unrecognised by the Protector himself. There is no foundation for the supposed connection of the Steward family with the royal house of Stuart. The descent of the Cromwells from "Glothian, Lord of Powis, before the Norman Conquest," is doubtless as mythical as the descent of the Stewards from "Banquo, the common ancestor of the Stewards and the Stuarts."

Both Cromwells and Stewards were families which had grown to wealth and importance at the dissolution of the monasteries. The Stewards had been planted at Ely, enriched with revenues of the Church, by the great-uncle of the Protector's mother, Robert Steward, D.D., who had the singular fortune to be for twenty years the last Catholic Prior, and then, for twenty years more, the first Protestant Dean, of Ely. The Cromwells of Huntingdon were descendants of Sir Richard Cromwell, otherwise called Williams, a kinsman of Thomas Cromwell, Earl of Essex, the *Malleus Monachorum* or "Hammer of Monasteries," under Henry VIII.

For generations the Cromwells were conspicuous for loyalty, chivalry, and public spirit. Sir Richard Cromwell, the founder of the house, the great-grandfather of the Protector, had been one of the *preux chevaliers* of Henry's Court, and was an ardent supporter of Thomas Cromwell, the Vicar-General. In letters to the Earl he signs himself "your bounden nephew"; he was, in fact, the son of Catherine, Cromwell's sister. Sir Richard's family was *Williams* of Glamorganshire, a name which he was authorised to change for that of his kinsman and patron; and in his will he describes himself as Sir Richard Williams, otherwise called Sir Richard Cromwell. His descendants continued to use the family name of Williams concurrently with that of Cromwell; it appears in Oliver's marriage settlement, and even in the inscription over the Protector's bed when his effigy lay in state. Sir Richard Cromwell retained the favour of Henry VIII. on the fall of his great kinsman. Honours, grants, offices, civil and military, came to him in profusion;

he married the daughter of Sir Thomas Martyn, Lord Mayor of London; and, dying one year before his master, he left vast estates in five counties to his children.

His eldest son, Sir Henry Cromwell, the Protector's grandfather, was knighted by Elizabeth in 1563, and in the next year entertained the Queen at Hinchinbrook, a noble house which he built on his principal estate, and in which he incorporated the suppressed Benedictine nunnery. He represented the county of Huntingdon in the Parliament of 1563, was four times High Sheriff, and by his liberality and magnificence acquired the name of the Golden Knight. He married a daughter of Sir Ralph Warren, Lord Mayor of London. Sir Oliver, the eldest son of Sir Henry, uncle and godfather to the Protector, was even more sumptuous and more loyal than his father and grandfather. He too was knighted by Elizabeth, served as High Sheriff for the counties of Huntingdon and Cambridge, and sat in many Parliaments in the reigns of the Queen, of James I., and of Charles I. He married first the daughter of Sir H. Bromley, Lord Chancellor, and afterwards the widow of Sir Horatio Palavicini, the famous financier. When James of Scotland succeeded to the throne of England, Sir Oliver entertained him during two days at Hinchinbrook on his state progress to London, with a lavish magnificence which delighted the king, and which was said to have surpassed any feast ever offered to monarch by a subject. He was made Knight of the Bath at the Coronation, and continuing his royal entertainments, he ultimately ruined himself; and lived in seclusion, a stubborn cavalier to the last, well into the Protectorate of his godson. The many sons of Sir Henry and those of Sir Oliver, all knights or country gentlemen in the eastern counties, served in public offices, in Parliament, or as soldiers; and, during the civil war, for the most part on the side of the king. The daughters of Sir Henry and those of Sir Oliver were married to men of good family and estate: the most illustrious of these being Oliver's aunt Elizabeth, the mother of John Hampden.

Robert Cromwell, the father of Oliver, was a cadet of this knightly house; and his simple home at Huntingdon was in modest contrast with the splendour of Hinchinbrook. As one of the younger sons of Sir Henry, the Golden Knight, he inherited a small estate, in and near the town of Huntingdon, chiefly possessions which formerly belonged to the Austin Canons. This estate amounted, with the great tithes of Hartford, to about £300 a year, a tolerable fortune in those times; rather more than £1000 now. His wife had a jointure of £60 a year, or somewhat more than £200 in our day. He represented the borough in Parliament in 1593; was one of the town bailiffs in two successive years; and was in the commission of the peace for the county. He lived in a stone house, at the northern extremity of the town, having extensive back premises and a fine garden, the Hinchin brook flowing through the courtyard. There Oliver was born. The room was to be seen until 1810; but the house has been twice rebuilt. It fronts the old Roman road, still called *Ermine Street*; and is now a solid manor-house with a fine old garden: some traces of the external walls and of the original offices remain. It is in the possession of Captain Isaac Bernard, and is known as *Cromwell House*: the footpath alongside its garden, leading to the water-meadows, is named *Cromwell's Walk*.

Robert Cromwell is described as a gentleman of good sense and competent learning; of a great spirit, but without any ambition; regular in his habits, reserved, and somewhat proud. He served in the local duties of his town and at quarter sessions, managed his estate, was on various commissions for draining the fens; a steadfast and worthy man, bringing up in honour a family of ten children, of whom Oliver was the only son that survived.

From the civil troubles to the present day controversy has raged round the question if he or his family carried on the trade of a brewer. Tradition, lampoons, and biographies persistently assert that he did; nor is there any real evidence to the contrary. The house at Huntingdon was occupied as a brewery before it belonged to Robert Cromwell; lampoons published during Charles I.'s lifetime certainly call Oliver a brewer; but his earliest, and most hostile, biographer asserts that not he but his father was the brewer. We are most circumstantially told that the brewing business was carefully managed by Mrs. Robert Cromwell, and continued by her on her husband's death. There is no decisive evidence; and the matter has no importance. Robert Cromwell, like his son Oliver, was a gentleman managing a small estate and cultivating a moderate farm. But the better opinion seems to be that the business of brewing was carried on at some time by Robert Cromwell, or his wife and widow; though not by Oliver himself.

Of Elizabeth Steward, the mother of Oliver, we have a record both clearer and more full. She was a granddaughter of Nicolas Steward, elder brother of the first Dean of Ely, who had secured for his family considerable estates in Ely, on long leases from the dean and chapter, together with the privilege of farming the great tithes. On the death of Elizabeth's father, her brother, Sir Thomas Steward, enjoyed the family estates: an energetic and popular citizen of Ely, who, being childless, regarded Oliver, the only son of his sister Elizabeth, as his heir. Elizabeth Steward, named of course, like Oliver's own wife and aunt, after the Queen, was the widow of William Lynne, when she married Robert Cromwell about 1591. By him she had ten children, of whom Oliver was the fifth. The concurrent testimony of all contemporary writers describes her as a woman of strong character, of sterling goodness, and of simple nature. The very lampoons and invectives have no evil word for this blameless matron. "Both Robert Cromwell and his wife," we are told, "were persons of great worth, . . . remarkable for living on a small fortune with decency, and maintaining a large family by their frugal circumspection." She survived her husband thirty-seven years, and married her daughters to men of worth and honour. She was much beloved by her relations, and also by those of her husband, particularly by Sir Oliver Cromwell, the godfather of her son. The supposed portrait of her shows us a face curiously resembling her son, the motherly form of the same type: strong, homely, keen, with firm mouth, penetrating eyes, a womanly goodness and peacefulness of expression; the genial face demurely enveloped in its flowing wimple and prim lawn kerchief. Between this Puritan mother and her great son love and esteem of the deepest continued till death. He was but eighteen in the year when she lost at once husband and father. From that time till her death mother and son lived almost constantly together. As her son rose to power she remained at his side to love, exhort, comfort; to pray for him and to fear for him. In the highest place, as in a humble place, she continued simple and steadfast. The Protector insisted on lodging her beside him in the Palace of Whitehall; and at her death, as it seems, in her ninetieth year, in spite of her wishes to the contrary, he buried her royally in the Abbey. There she lay in peace amongst kings and queens until the Restoration, when her bones were cast forth and thrust into a hole. Few English women have had a destiny more strange: yet in all things she remained the homely, provident, devout matron. "A little while before her death," says Thurloe, "she gave my lord her blessing in these words: 'The Lord cause His face to shine upon you, and comfort you in all your adversities, and enable you to do great things for the glory of your Most High God, and to be a relief unto His people. My dear son, I leave my heart with thee. A good-night!'"

Of such father and mother, and from such a home, came Oliver, the future Protector of the Commonwealth. Born, as we have said, on the 25th April 1599, he was christened in the church of St. John's, at Huntingdon, as the parish register still records, on the 29th of that month; and Sir Oliver, his uncle, gave him his name at the font. Not a few of the elements which make up the history of our people were represented in his birth and surroundings. Essentially a townsman, the son of a townsman, one who passed his early life in towns, but also a landowner occupied in the business of farming, he lived to maturity, as his father had done, the active citizen of a thriving eastern township. The eastern townships then were the core of the prosperous, independent, and pious middle class; and the household of Robert Cromwell in Huntingdon was a type of that order of life. Oliver Cromwell belonged to a race which, by its wealth and alliances, stood in the front rank of the untitled gentry of England, and which, by its ostentatious loyalty, had been personally connected with the Court for three generations. Hinchinbrook, with its royal pageants and knightly splendour, was within a mile of Robert Cromwell's plain home in Huntingdon. The uncles and great-uncles, the sisters, aunts, and great aunts of Oliver were connected by their marriages with scores of families conspicuous in honour and the service of the State. His father's paternal estate, and that of his mother's brother, both of which Oliver inherited and farmed, were old Church lands. Cromwells and Stewards, whoever their remoter ancestors might have been, were conspicuous examples of the new Reformation houses. The homestead in which Oliver was born had been built on the ruins of the Augustine friars; the lordly mansion of his grandfather had for its domestic offices the cells of Benedictine nuns. On every circumstance of his home the Protestant seal was set. So many things went to the making of that compound nature—knighthood, burgerhood, the Crown's honours, the State's service, the ancient Church, the Reformation, revolution both social and religious, Puritanism, the Bible.

For Oliver's boyhood there is nothing but unlimited conjecture and most dubious legend. Neither of these need detain us. In January 1603 Sir Henry Cromwell, the Golden Knight, died at Hinchinbrook, and Sir Oliver, his son, reigned in his stead. In March died Elizabeth, the last of the Tudors, and James, first of the Stuarts, peacefully succeeded. In April, two days after the boy's fourth birthday, took place the royal entertainment which Sir Oliver gave to the new king. Passing through the sculptured gatehouse of the Benedictine convent, James entered the great court of Hinchinbrook in state, Lord Southampton bearing before him the sword of honour presented by the town of Huntingdon; the dignitaries of the University came from Cambridge to congratulate the king in a Latin oration. The mansion was thrown open; all comers were made free of its kitchens and cellars; and when, on the third day, the king set forth to his capital, a gold cup, horses, hounds, hawks, and gifts of money were presented to James and to his Scotch courtiers. The earliest recollections of the child must have been of the new gay dynasty, and his own courtly godfather.

There is a tradition that in the following year Charles, then Duke of York, was taken to Hinchinbrook on his way to London, that he played with the little Oliver, and was worsted in fisticuffs. In 1601 Oliver was five and Charles was four: it is quite possible that they met as children in Sir Oliver's hall. But enough of this and of the other traditions of his boyhood. How the ape at Hinchinbrook carried him oft as an infant on to the roof; how he was saved from drowning by the curate, who lived to repent his act; how he robbed orchards and dove-houses, and was known as an "apple-dragon"; how he had nightly visions and prophetic omens; how he played rude pranks at Yule-tide; how Sir Oliver had him ducked by the Lord of Misrule; how Sir Thomas Steward rebuked him as a traitor; how, when one night a spirit appeared to him in a dream and foretold that he should be the greatest man in the kingdom, his father had him mercilessly caned; how "from his infancy to his childhood he was of a cross and peevish disposition"; how, in a school play, he had once to put on a stage crown and to say—

> "Methinks I hear my noble parasites
> Styling me Caesar or great Alexander,"

—are not these things written in the "Lives," lampoons, and loose flux called "tradition"—part, it may be, truth, part exaggeration, part scurrilous invention?

One certain and important fact stands out in Oliver's boyhood. He was sent to the free school at Huntingdon, an ancient foundation attached to the Hospital of St. John, which still flourishes and retains some fragments of the old twelfth-century chapel. The then master and warden was Thomas Beard, Doctor of Divinity. The connection between Oliver and his master was very close and very long; and of the latter we have very definite knowledge. For upwards of thirty years, and down to his death in 1632, Dr. Beard lived, taught, and preached in Huntingdon. He was not only master and warden of St. John's foundation, but "lecturer" in All Saints' Church, and also an active citizen and justice of the peace in Huntingdon. He is the author of several works—*Anti-Christ the Pope of Rome*, etc., *The Theatre of God's Judgments*, etc. etc., and a Latin play; from all of which we gather that he was a sound scholar, a man of wide reading, a zealous Puritan, and an ardent reformer. His reputed portrait, holding his ferule, is that of a stern, vigorous, keen man. Gossip represents him as a flogging pedagogue, under whom the young Oliver suffered much and to little purpose. It may be so, it may be not. What we know is, that Dr. Beard is constantly associated in Huntingdon records with the Cromwells, that he witnesses Robert's will, that he was Oliver's first teacher, that Oliver's earliest extant letter is an earnest plea for such lectures which "provide for the feeding of souls," and his first speech in Parliament was to bear witness of this very Dr. Beard, that the Doctor and Oliver are two of the three justices for Huntingdon. The future Protector then, we know, was educated in the Grammar School of his native town by a typical Puritan teacher, with whom he remained in close intimacy till manhood.

From the Grammar School of Huntingdon Oliver Cromwell proceeded to Cambridge, where he was admitted on the 23rd of April 1616 as Fellow-Commoner at Sidney Sussex College. It was the very day on which Shakespeare died at Stratford. It was within two days of young Cromwell's seventeenth birthday. Sidney Sussex College was stigmatised by Laud as one of the nurseries of Puritanism. The head then and for twenty-seven years afterwards was Dr. Samuel Ward, one of the translators of the English Bible in 1611, who was named in 1618 as one of the delegates at the Synod of Dort. Once accounted a Puritan, he was always a stout Protestant, a man of great learning, morbidly sensitive as to his duty, a strict disciplinarian, who records in his diary his compunction for the sin of too great laxity in exacting from his scholars accounts of the sermons they attended. There is no evidence how long Cromwell's college career lasted. The unfriendly "Lives" assure us it was short. He took no degree, nor does his name appear elsewhere in the books.

How far did Cromwell's studies at school and at college extend? The unfriendly memoirs assert that he gained little at either; that, on the contrary, he was more famous in the fields than in the schools; that he was foremost in football, cudgels, and all boisterous sports; nay, that he consorted with drinking companions, gained the name of royster, and was given to debauchery. The friendly memoirs, on the other hand, assure us that he made "good proficiency in the university"; "that there wanted not presages of his future greatness"; that "he finished his course of study, and perfectly acquired the Latin tongue"; that he excelled chiefly in mathematics, and "yielded to no gentleman in the rest of the arts and sciences." One of them, indeed, tells us that "he was not so much addicted to speculation as to action, as was observed by his tutor." That is, perhaps, at once friendly and truthful.

The truth as to Cromwell's learning is probably this. He

certainly understood Latin conversation. Latin was then the language of diplomacy; and educated men were supposed to use it readily both in writing and speech. Beverning carried on a negotiation with the Protector speaking in Latin. Burnet says that Cromwell spoke Latin, but viciously and scantily; perhaps as many of our statesmen now speak French. In letters in mature life Cromwell spoke of his son's education; he recommends to him history, to study mathematics, cosmography. "These fit for public services for which a man is born." He tells Richard he should recreate himself with Raleigh's *History of the World*. Now a man who loved such books as Raleigh's *History of the World* and Dr. Beard's *Theatre of God's Judgments*, a book with a curious range of miscellaneous reading, would have a considerable storehouse of historical analogies. Edmund Waller, the poet, declared that Cromwell "was very well read in Greek and Roman story." From his letters and speeches we gather that he had a well-stored mind, and we are told that, as Protector, he collected "a noble collection of books." There is no reason to suppose that he ever was a student in the special sense of the word. But he acquired, at some time of his life, an education adequate for all his public duties.

It is probable that Oliver's college career did not extend beyond his eighteenth year, a year which proved an epoch in his life. In the March of that year (1617) King James was entertained at Hinchinbrook for the fourth and last time, and was attended by Laud and by Buckingham. On the 6th of June following Robert Cromwell made his will; on the 24th he was buried. On the 20th of the month, four days before the burial, his daughter Margaret, then just seventeen, was married to Valentine Walton. We know no more of the circumstances under which Oliver within four days was called on to attend his young sister's wedding and then his father's funeral. By his will Robert Cromwell left two-thirds of his estate, and a sum of £600, to his wife for twenty-one years to maintain his daughters. Of these he left six living, the youngest about seven years old. Oliver, his only son, was then eighteen. It seems that, being his father's heir, and the only son of his mother, he did not continue at college. He probably returned to his home at Huntingdon, at least for a time, to manage his father's estate.

A persistent but confused tradition asserts that Cromwell, after leaving college, studied law at Lincoln's Inn; and it is even said that he occupied rooms in the fine old gatehouse of 1518. His name is not found in the books of any Inn; but it is difficult to resist the repeated assertion of the "Lives," and still more the inscription over his effigy as it lay in state, that "he was educated in Cambridge, afterwards of Lincoln's Inn." It is extremely probable that he made some study of law, as did every civilian who had any idea of entering public life, as did Eliot, Pym, Hampden. When, how long, and to what purpose he studied law, we know nothing. There are indications in his speeches that he understood the general principles of law, and he is said to have carried on a long legal argument with learned civilians, whom he impressed with his knowledge.

Such was the course of his education to full age. The times had not a little to teach him. He was six years old when the Gunpowder Plot shook all England; eleven when Henry IV. was stabbed in Paris. In his twelfth year appeared the new version of the Bible. The whole book-learning of the youth must have gone on at the very season when that incomparable masterpiece of the English tongue was beginning to mould the speech and thought of our race. When he was nineteen Raleigh was beheaded in Old Palace Yard, a sacrifice to Spain; and in the same year began the terrible Thirty Years' War in Germany, dragging on its devastating course until the end of our first Civil War in England.

What was the manner of life of the young man we know not. Friendly writers tell us that he was addicted more to the reading of men than to poring over authors. Unfriendly writers assure us (but in a confused, inconsistent way) that he was given to roystering, extravagance, coarseness, and vice. Such testimony as theirs we cannot trust; but we cannot now refute it. Certainly he bore through life a strange turn for rough jests. When we first reach authentic utterances of Cromwell himself, we meet with a spirit of intense religious earnestness. The whole of his surroundings in childhood and youth tended to that direction. A Puritan mother, a serious father, a zealous Puritan schoolmaster, a Puritan college, under a Puritan head, his father's premature death and his own early responsibilities, his veneration for his mother, his early marriage, do not suggest a vicious youth. Yet they do not positively exclude it. At the age of thirty-nine he writes to his cousin, Mrs. St. John: "You know what my manner of life hath been. Oh, I lived in and loved darkness, and hated light; I was a chief, the chief of sinners." So, indeed, said St. Paul. And in the mouth of an earnest Puritan this phrase from Scripture refers, not to profligacy, but to a time before "conversion." That he should so write at thirty-nine suggests that his spiritual conversion was not in early youth. When and how that conversion took place we know not. There was a time, no doubt, when that mighty nature had not fully absorbed the great Bible conception, how the entire life of man is one intimate communion with God. There may have been a period (we have no sufficient proof that there was) when that passionate mass of manhood may have been a law to itself, in the lust of the flesh, and the lust of the eyes, and the pride of life. Each of us must imagine as he best can how that great soul passed into its new birth, at what age, under what surroundings, and through what agonies and storms.

CHAPTER II

MARRIAGE – FAMILY – DOMESTIC LIFE

A.D. 1620–1628. AETAT. 21–29

On the 22nd of August 1620 Oliver Cromwell was married to Elizabeth Bourchier, in St. Giles's, Cripplegate, in London—the church where fifty-four years later John Milton was buried. In this year Milton, aged twelve, entered as scholar at St. Paul's School. Oliver was twenty-one years and four months old on his wedding-day. His wife, who was one year older, was a daughter of Sir James Bourchier, a knight and wealthy merchant of Tower Hill, London, having an estate at Felsted in Essex, where he ordinarily resided. The Bourchiers of the city, we are told, were in no way related to the feudal Bourchiers, Earls of Essex, nor to Sir John Bourchier, one of the king's judges. Little is known of the family, and they do not appear in the history of the time. We are told that the Bourchiers were connections of the Hampdens, and that Oliver owed his wife to the introduction of his aunt, Elizabeth Hampden.

Her portrait shows us a pleasant, not uncomely woman, with much dignity of expression, very far from a Puritan. We take her to be a quiet, affectionate, sensible woman, without much character or power, un willing at first to assume the position in the State which awaited her, but reconciling herself to it without much difficulty, and playing her part in it without scandal or offence.

Three letters of Oliver's to her remain, and one of hers to him. They are affectionate, trustful, and natural; Biblical in phrase. On her side, she complains (unreasonably enough), during his northern campaign, that he does not write more frequently; on his, he protests his public duties. Thirty years after their marriage he can write to her (the day after Dunbar): "Truly, if I love you not too well, I think I err not on the other hand much. Thou art dearer to me than any creature; let that suffice." And she writes to him: "Truly my life is but half a life in your absence." He does not seem to have felt for her judgment the profound veneration that he showed to his mother. We do not gather the impression that she was a woman of much distinction. The lampoons, of course, are as brutal towards her as towards him. She brought up her daughters to be women of good breeding and nice feeling. Nor is there any reason to doubt but that she was a worthy woman, doing her duty to the best of her powers, to husband, children, and friends.

Sir James Bourchier, the father of Mrs. Cromwell, was a man of wealth; but it does not appear what fortune she had. On his side, Oliver Cromwell settled on his wife for her life the parsonage house at Hartford, with the glebe lands and tithes in the county of Huntingdon. To Huntingdon, to his mother's house, he took his bride; and there for eleven years they lived together—only son, his wife and children, with the widowed mother and her unmarried daughters. Of this period of his life there is almost no record, save the birth and baptism of his children, until we come to his entrance into public life, when he was sent to Parliament in 1628 to represent the borough of Huntingdon. After one short year of Parliament he returned again to private life, until the re-opening of the great Parliamentary struggle in 1640. The public career of Oliver Cromwell shall be reserved for future chapters. Here are the main outlines of his private life.

In 1631 he sold his paternal estate in Huntingdon and removed to St. Ives, where he leased lands which he farmed for five years. In 1636 he removed to Ely; and there he farmed the lands left to him by his uncle, Sir Thomas Steward. There his mother and sisters rejoined him. Thus, with the short break of the Parliament of 1628–29, the quiet domestic life of Oliver Cromwell continued for twenty years (1620–40), from his marriage in his twenty-second year until his own forty-second year. Here till long past middle age, in this "sequester'd vale of life," he kept the noiseless tenor of his way—

> in "his private gardens, where
> He lived reserved and austere."

It seems convenient here, before we enter on the clash of Parliament and war, to collect the few incidents worth noting in the family and personal story of the future Protector. By his wife, Elizabeth Bourchier, Oliver Cromwell had nine children, of whom they reared four sons and four daughters.[1] All, except the youngest, were baptized at Huntingdon. The four sons were all educated at Felsted School, in Essex, the place where their grandfather lived—a school that reared some famous scholars, and which still flourishes. Robert, the eldest, died there at the age of seventeen. Oliver, the second, was a captain in the Civil War, and died in service at the age of twenty-one. Richard, the third son, succeeded his father as Protector, and died quietly at the age of eighty-six, in the reign of Anne. Henry, the fourth son, served in the war, was Lord Deputy in Ireland, and died in 1674. Of the daughters, Bridget became the wife of General Ireton, and afterwards of General Fleetwood. Elizabeth, married to John Claypole, died four weeks before her father. Mary, married to Lord Fauconberg, she whom Swift knew and called "handsome and like her father," died at the age of seventy-five. Frances, married to Robert Rich, grandson and heir of the Earl of Warwick, afterwards married Sir

1 [One son died in infancy.]

John Russell, Baronet, eldest brother of Henry Cromwell's wife, and died at the age of eighty-two. The widow of the Protector survived him many years, and died in obscurity at the age of seventy-four.

Of these eight children, three—Henry, Bridget, and Frances—left ultimate descendants. Richard, the Protector's successor, married Dorothy Mayor, of Hursley, and they had nine children, but no grandchildren. Henry, the Protector's fourth son, married Elizabeth, daughter of Sir Francis Russell, Baronet, of Chippenham, by whom he had seven children. Their descendants were numerous and are still flourishing. The male line was continued down to living memory. Oliver Cromwell, the last male descendant of that name, died in 1821; and his daughter, Elizabeth Oliveria Russell, who died in 1849, was the last descendant of the Protector born a Cromwell. The descendants in the female line, both of Henry and of Bridget, are still plentiful. Frances, the youngest child of the Protector, by her second husband, Sir John Russell, Baronet, of Chippenham, had five children. From these there are still descendants of the Protector in the female lines too numerous to recount, and in families of the highest rank.[2]

Four of the five sisters of Oliver in these quiet years married men of their own rank and position. Margaret married Colonel Valentine Walton, one of Charles I.'s judges. Anna became Mrs. Sewster; her daughter married Sir William Lockhart. Catherine married Colonel Jones, another of the king's judges, and himself afterwards executed. Jane married General Desborough, one of the generals of the Commonwealth. Robina married Dr. French, and afterwards Dr. Wilkins, Bishop of Chester, one of the founders of the Royal Society; her daughter married Archbishop Tillotson.

What manner of man in all these years was the unknown great captain and ruler? Three qualities especially stand out.

2 [See Appendix A.]

Deep family affection; tenderness towards sufferers; Bible religion. Every fragment of record from his private life tells one or other of these. In the range of great characters in history there are some in whom the passion for social justice burned as keenly as in Cromwell; but there are few, indeed, in whom the family affections nourish a spirit so pure in the midst of distracting public duties to the last hour of an over-burdened life. There is certainly no ruler since Saint Louis in whom the personal communion with God is a consciousness so vivid and habitual.

"He was naturally compassionate towards objects in distress, even to an effeminate measure," wrote John Maidston. Long before he was known to the nation, he was marked in his own country as the friend of the suffering and oppressed; he did "exceed in tenderness towards sufferers." His house became the refuge of persecuted ministers; he stoutly maintained their cause, and strove to secure them their stipends. His farming, the Royalist writers tell us, suffered from his habit of gathering his labourers twice a day around him, and praying with them, and discoursing to them. For years before the Civil War the future Protector of the Commonwealth had become known far and wide as the village-Hampden with the dauntless breast.

Of Cromwell's love for his wife and for his mother we have spoken. To his wife he writes in his Scotch campaign:

> "Thou art dearer to me than any creature. . . . Pray for me; truly I do daily for thee and the dear Family. . . . My love to the dear little ones; I pray for grace for them. I thank them for their Letters; let me have them often. ... If Dick Cromwell and his Wife be with you, my dear love to them. I pray for them: they shall, God willing, hear from me. I love them very dearly.—Truly I am not able as yet to write much. I am weary; and rest, Thine,

To Bridget Ireton he writes (he forty-seven, she twenty-two):

> "Who ever tasted that the Lord is gracious, without some sense of self, vanity, and badness? Who ever tasted that graciousness of His, and could go less [become weaker] in desire—less than pressing after full enjoyment? Dear Heart, press on; let not Husband, let not anything cool thy affections after Christ. I hope he will be an occasion to inflame them. That which is best worthy of love in thy Husband is that of the image of Christ he bears. Look on that, and love it best, and all the rest for that. I pray for thee and him; do so for me."

Bridget Ireton and Elizabeth Claypole were apparently the daughters of his deepest confidence. But it is on his poor son, Richard, that the father's care seems chiefly bestowed. With regard to Richard he had no illusions. The father well knew the feebleness, indolence, the lightness of nature of the son. Yet he is continually stirring him to better things, seeking to place him under the highest influences. To Richard Mayor, Richard Cromwell's father-in-law, on the son's marriage, he writes (1649):

> "I have delivered my son up to you; and I hope you will counsel him: he will need it; and, indeed, I believe he likes well what you say, and will be advised by you. I wish he may be serious; the times require it."

Again he writes to Mayor:

> "I have committed my Son to you; pray give him advice. I envy him not his contents; but I fear he should be swallowed up in them. I would have him mind and understand Business, read a little History, study the Mathematics and Cosmography:—these are good, with subordination to the things of God. Better than Idleness, or mere outward worldly contents. These fit for Public services, for which a man is born."

To his son, Richard, he writes, during the fierce campaign in Ireland:—

> "DICK CROMWELL—I take your Letters kindly: I like

expressions when they come plainly from the heart, and are not strained nor affected.

"I am persuaded it's the Lord's mercy to place you where you are: I wish you may own it and be thankful, fulfilling all relations to the glory of God. Seek the Lord and His face continually—let this be the business of your life and strength, and let all things be subservient and in order to this! You cannot find nor behold the face of God but in Christ; therefore labour to know God in Christ; which the Scripture makes to be the sum of all, even Life Eternal. Because the true knowledge is not literal or speculative; but inward; transforming the mind to it. . . .

"Take heed of an inactive vain spirit! Recreate yourself with Sir Walter Raleigh's *History*: it's a body of History, and will add much more to your understanding than fragments of Story. — Intend to understand the Estate I have settled; it's your concernment to know it all, and how it stands. I have heretofore suffered much by too much trusting others. I know my Brother Mayor will be helpful to you in all this.

"You will think, perhaps, I need not advise you To love your Wife! The Lord teach you how to do it—or else it will be done ill-favouredly. Though Marriage be no instituted Sacrament; yet where the undefiled bed is, and love, this union aptly resembles 'that of' Christ and His Church. If you can truly love your Wife, what 'love' doth Christ bear to His Church and every poor soul therein—who 'gave Himself' for it, and to it!—Commend me to your Wife; tell her I entirely love her, and rejoice in the goodness of the Lord to her. I wish her everyway fruitful. I thank her for her loving Letter." . . .

Three times that great heart was wrung with agony on the death of a beloved child. Robert, his eldest son, named after Oliver's own father, died in his eighteenth year at Felsted, May 1639. The parish register still records (one thinks in the words dictated by the father), *Et Robertus fuit eximiè pius juvenis, Deum timens supra multos*—"Now Robert was a youth of singular piety, fearing God more than ordinary." Nineteen years afterwards, fresh from his daughter's deathbed, almost on his own deathbed, the broken-hearted father recurred again to this his first great loss. He had read to him those verses in Philippians which end: "I can do all things through Christ which strengtheneth me" (Phil. iv. 13); and then he said: "This Scripture did once save my life; when my eldest son died; which went as a dagger to my heart, indeed it did." Again, death struck down his second son, Oliver, who died of smallpox at Newport Pagnell, just before Marston. To this loss he seems to recur in the noble letter to Colonel Walton on the field of Marston Moor reporting the death of his son in battle. "Sir, God hath taken away your eldest son. . . . Sir, you know my own trials in this way, but the Lord supported me with this, that the Lord took him into the happiness we all pant for and live for."

The third great loss, the most cruel of all, undoubtedly hastened the Protector's end. On the 6th of August 1658 his favourite daughter, Elizabeth Claypole, died. "She had great sufferings," we are told, "great exercises of spirit." Thurloe writes: "For the last fourteen days his Highness has been by her bedside at Hampton Court, unable to attend to any public business whatever. ... It was observed that his sense of her outward misery in the pains she endured, took deep impression on him; who, indeed, was ever a most indulgent and tender father." And then a few days after came that outburst of grief as he thought of the death of his first-born. In three weeks more he was dying himself. For the thirty-eight years of his married life, Cromwell was all that a loving husband and father could be: overflowing with affection, even on the battlefield, and in the stress of affairs; indulgent, but not weak; considerate, provident, just; counselling, reproving, exhorting; yearning to lead his children to feel his own intense sense of God's presence.

The passages from his letters already given are enough to show how profoundly Cromwell's nature was saturated with Biblical theology. He was a Puritan of the Puritans; full of the dominant idea of personal salvation by faith; his whole imagination and speech were steeped in the language of the Bible, as expounded by Calvin. Never were the thought and the expression of any people more powerfully transformed than were the thought and language of England by the translation of the Bible. The issue of the Authorised Version, and still more the multiplication of portable editions of Scripture, affected our people as hardly any book in the world ever affected a nation. The years of Cromwell's life exactly kept pace with the growth, culmination, and waning of this first intense influence. In the next century England had a large and rich printed literature. But in Cromwell's youth the Catholic manuals had been thrust out, and English literature as yet was not, or was not yet open to the people. The Bible was almost the sole poetry, the sole morality, the sole religion, familiar to all and accessible in print. Its mighty imagery, its majestic utterances as to man's soul and God's power, its mystical ecstasy, its scheme of sin and death, of future life and judgment, of man's vileness, and the nothingness of this transitory life, wrought into the core of the finest and deepest natures of the age. Milton, Lucy Hutchinson, have given us a measure of this spirit in its beauty and harmony. Fox and Bunyan give us a sense of its mysticism and its passion. But no man in that age drank it into his whole nature with more intense reality than did Cromwell.

It is very hard for any of us to-day rightly to grasp all this. There are still Bible Christians, not a few: men and women, to whom the Word of God is ever ringing in their ears, day and night continually; to whom every word, thought, and act, of themselves as of others, is felt to be, moment by moment, an irrevocable step to a real heaven or to a real hell. But they who so live are the few. The world around them visibly goes on with no such absorbing sense of God's purposes and God's judgments. They live in a world of their own; puzzled, half-paralysed, hoping all things, believing all things, but not outwardly triumphant. The social and mental environment round them is visibly alien to the kingdom of heaven in which they hope and believe; wherein they move and have their being. And not a few of us find mental, moral, historical obstacles in the way of any such Biblical belief, or Biblical hopes; and we are not struck dead, nor are we branded and pilloried, nor even are we outcasts and strangers; but we are the dear friends, children, parents, brothers, and sisters of those who live by the Gospel alone.

But in the lifetime of Oliver Cromwell the society in which he lived had absorbed to the depths of their souls this Biblical conception of life. Their Bible was literally food to their understanding and a guide to their conduct. They saw the visible finger of God in every incident of life; they heard the authentic voice of God in every turn of existence. They saw Satan in everything evil, and heard the noise of devils in all that was harmful, vicious, or unjust. If they took counsel of each other of their own judgment, they literally believed that God and His angels prompted every thought. If one seemed to them just and useful, he was beloved of God; if one seemed to do harm, he was hated of God. If they were undecided, they sought God. If they felt confidence, they had found God. If they felt hopeless, they had lost God. To be living an honest life was simply to be conscious of unbroken communion with God's spirit. Now that which in our day devout men and women come to feel in their earnest moments of prayer, the devout Puritan felt, as a second nature, in his rising up and in his lying down; in the market-place and in the home, in society and business; in Parliament, in council, and on the field of battle. He felt in the full tide of daily life what pious men now feel on their knees and on their deathbed.

And feeling this, the Puritan had no shame in uttering it, in the very words of the Bible wherein he had learned so to feel; nay, he would have burned with shame had he faltered in using those words. It is very hard for us now to grasp what this implies. After a few generations the Biblical terms ceased to sound as the very words in which God had spoken, but grew to be mere customary phrases; they became the dialect of an order of men; they grew to be a fashion; they were imitated; and soon withered up into a cant. But there was a generation in which this phraseology was the natural speech of men, to whom the Bible was their sole literature, poetry, and religion. Oliver Cromwell grew to manhood in the very centre of that generation. Towards the close of his life that Biblical language was already the external shibboleth of a sect. He had not that sense of poetic harmony which prevented Milton from adopting it. That he chose to retain it through life has heavily weighted his memory, and has retarded by centuries the understanding of his character. From manhood to his deathbed Oliver Cromwell used no other English, spoken or written, save the Biblical dialect. To him it was no dialect; but the literal assertion of truths which he felt to the roots of his being. When Cromwell wrote "Here is the hand of God," he literally did think the Creator of all things had so appointed it to be. When he "sought the Lord," he did literally believe himself to be in communion with God, to be receiving His direct command. When he said that "God had given them the victory," he meant this in its literal sense, as fully as did Joshua or Moses. It is a melancholy thought that the utterances of the most sincere of men in the innocency of their hearts should now be repulsive to us, simply because insincere men chose to imitate their words, and to build up into a cant what was once heartfelt truthfulness.

This is not the place to pass judgment on the Puritan's way of using his Bible, or his general scheme of religion. It is sufficient for us that Oliver Cromwell accepted it wholly: in its narrowness and its strength, with all its good, and not a little of its evil. Few men in our age look on every circumstance of their daily lives as arranged by an inexhaustible set of special providences; nor do they think every impulse which crosses their minds to be the work of direct inspiration. To the modern psychologist this singular type of theological exaltation amounts in effect to the kindling into intense activity the whole moral nature. This ecstatic communion with God in practice resulted in a hyper-aesthesia of the conscience and the will. The zealot who felt himself in hourly communion with the Divine will was really consulting his own highest standard of the Just and the True. When he sought God, he was probing his understanding to its depths. When he had found assurance, his resolve was fixed down to the very roots of his soul. And thus it depended very much on the zealot's own nature whether the result was good or bad. A great and wise man had his greatness and his sagacity intensified, for his own soul was transfigured to himself. A man of self-reliance had his will heated to a white heat, for he knew himself to be the chosen instrument to work out the decrees of the Almighty. The brave man became insensible to any form of danger; the unselfish man became the type of self-devotion; the compassionate man boiled with hate of whatever was unjust, whatever gave pain. And so the cruel man lost all trace of human pity; the selfish man lost all shame; the self-sufficient man treated all who opposed him as the enemies of God; the hypocrite found ready to his hand a whole apparatus of deceit; the traitor found current a complete code of villainy. It is for this reason that Puritanism and the Puritans have often been described in the language of extravagant praise and extravagant blame. The greater Puritans deserved the praise; the worse deserved the blame. It was a form of belief which could bring out all the good and all the evil of the heart. It made some noble natures heroic; it made some base natures devilish. Men may doubt if the good or the evil preponderated in the scheme as a whole. Men can hardly doubt that it infused into the greater natures which it mastered, a solemnity and a power such as have but once or twice been equalled in the whole history of mankind.

The Calvinistic theology did not sink into Cromwell's soul without a great shock to his character and health. Bunyan has left us a memorable picture of the first consciousness of sin. "My sins," he says, "did so offend the Lord, that even in my childhood He did scare and affright me with fearful dreams, and did terrify me with dreadful visions." Cromwell, we are told, had been given to visions from his childhood; and this mood seems to have deepened in manhood into a religious form of hypochondria. Sir Philip Warwick tells us that Dr. Simcott, Cromwell's physician at Huntingdon, assured him, "that for many years his Patient was a most splenetick man, and had phansyes about the cross in that town; and that he had been called up to him at midnight and such unreasonable hours very many times, upon a strong phansy, which made him believe he was then dying "; and Sir Philip gives the common story of his conversion, and says that, "he joyned himself to men of his own temper, who pretended unto transports and revelations." And it is thought that this is confirmed by an entry in the diary of Sir Theodore Mayerne, the famous Court physician, who prescribed (15th September 1628) for "Mons. Cromwell, *valde melancholicus*."

Into this religious melancholy of his we have a profound insight by that memorable letter to his cousin, Mrs. St. John (October 1638):

> "Truly no poor creature hath more cause to put himself forth in the cause of his God than I. I have had plentiful wages beforehand; and I am sure I shall never earn the least mite. The Lord accept me in His Son, and give me to walk in the light, — and give us to walk in the light, as He is the light! He it is that enlighteneth our blackness, our darkness. I dare not say, He hideth His face from me. He giveth me to see light in His light. One beam in a dark place hath exceeding much refreshment in it:—blessed be His Name for shining upon so dark a heart as mine! You know what my manner of life hath been. Oh, I lived in

> and loved darkness, and hated light; I was a chief, the chief of sinners. This is true: I hated godliness, yet God had mercy on me. O the riches of His mercy! Praise Him for me;—that He who hath begun a good work would perfect it in the day of Christ."

Thus passed the years of Cromwell's private life in his native town and county—in the rearing of a large family of children; in farming his paternal acres; in gathering round him the godly, the labouring, and the afflicted; in intimacy with the Hampdens, St. Johns, and many other Puritan families of his kindred; in service as borough magistrate and bailiff; in maintaining the cause of the "lecturers" and other preachers of the Gospel; in melancholy communings of soul, amidst the lonely reaches of the sluggish Ouse, as to the Judgment to come and the state of this land on earth.

What was the outward man in whom this spirit dwelt? Of few persons in history has the portraiture been preserved in a way more perfect and authentic. He had a tall, powerful frame, strong of limb, well knit, somewhat heavy. A large square head, and a countenance massive, and far from refined, his enemies said, swollen and red. That face has been preserved for us in the portraits of Cooper, Walker, Faithorne, and Lely; in all with singular resemblance.[3] Of them all Cooper was the most successful. No human countenance recorded is more familiar to us than that broad, solid face with the thick and prominent red nose; the heavy gnarled brow, with its historic wart; eyes firm, penetrating, sad; square jaw and close-set mouth; scanty tufts of hair on lip and chin; long, loose brown locks flowing down in waves on to the shoulder. His whole air breathing energy, firmness, passion, pity, and sorrow—

> "his face
> Deep scars of thunder had intrencht, and care
> Sat on his faded cheek, but under brows

3 [See Appendix B.]

Of dauntless courage."

There is a famous sketch of him, as he first appeared in public, by Sir Philip Warwick, a royalist of sense and not unfair:

> "The first time that ever I took notice of him was in the very beginning of the Parliament held in November 1640, when I vainly thought myself a courtly young Gentleman (for we Courtiers valued ourselves much upon our good clothes): I came one morning into the House well clad, and perceived a Gentleman speaking (whom I knew not) very ordinarily apparelled; for it was a plain cloth-suit, which seemed to have been made by an ill country-tailor; his linen was plain, and not very clean; and I remember a speck or two of blood upon his little band, which was not much larger than his collar; his hat was without a hat-band; his stature was of a good size, his sword stuck close to his side, his countenance swollen and reddish, his voice sharp and untuneable, and his eloquence full of fervour.". . .

And Sir Philip goes on to say how he lived to see this very gentleman "appear of a great and majestic deportment and comely" presence.

A counterpart to this picture is the Puritan sketch of the Protector, written by John Maidston to Governor Winthrop:

> "His body was well compact and strong, his stature under six feet (I believe about two inches), his head so shaped as you might see it a storehouse and shop both of a vast treasury of natural parts. His temper exceeding fiery, as I have known, but the flame of it kept down for the most part, or soon allayed by those moral endowments he had. He was naturally compassionate towards objects in distress, even to an effeminate measure; though God had made him a heart, wherein was left little room for any fear, but what was due to himself, of which there was a large proportion. Yet did he exceed in tenderness towards sufferers. A larger soul, I think, hath seldom dwelt in a house of clay than his was."

Such was the man whom, in his twenty-eighth year, his

fellow-citizens of Huntingdon chose to represent them in Parliament—17th March 1628.

The public life of Oliver Cromwell had now begun.

Appendix A

It is a curious example of the persistence of the English governing families, and of their close intermarriages, that the blood of Oliver Cromwell still runs through female lines in the veins of the following well-known persons:—Marquis of Ripon, Earls of Chichester, Morley, Clarendon, Cowper, heir-presumptive to the earldom of Derby, Lord Ampthill, Lord Walsingham, Countess of Rothes, Mr. Charles Villiers, M.P., Sir John Lubbock, M.P., Sir F. W. Frankland, Sir Charles Strickland, Sir H. E. F. Lewis, Sir W. Worsley, Sir W. Payne-Gallwey, the Astleys of Checkers Court, the Polhills of Kent, the Tennants of Glamorganshire, the families of Vyner, Lister, Berners, Nicholas, Gosset, Prescott, Field, Mr. S. R. Gardiner, the historian, etc. During the present century at least seven persons descended from the Protector have held office under the Crown, including one Prime Minister, Lord Goderich; one Foreign Secretary, Lord Clarendon; two Lords-Lieutenant of Ireland, and a Viceroy in India. Amongst those who have married descendants of Cromwell are the Earls of Darnley, Lytton, Lathom, Lord Stanley of Preston, Sir W. Harcourt, M.P., Sir A. Borthwick, M.P., Mr. Samuel Whitbread, M.P. The late Sir George Cornewall Lewis, the statesman and author, was a descendant of the Protector; and Lady Theresa Lewis, his wife, author of a work in illustration of Lord Clarendon, was a descendant at once of Oliver the Protector and of Edward Hyde the Chancellor. I am informed by a lady, one of the descendants of the Protector, that it was usual in her family to keep the 30th of January as a day of humiliation and prayer. They were taught as children that an ancestral visitation hung over them, which would certainly overtake them in this world or the next. Some of the Cromwells resumed the name of *Williams* after the Restoration. The arms of the Cromwells, as shown at Hinchinbrook, are *Sable, a lion rampant, argent.* Crest, *a demi-lion rampant argent, in his dexter gamb a gem-ring, or.* The latter is said to have been granted to Sir Richard Cromwell by Henry VIII., when he gave the knight his diamond ring in reward for splendid feats performed in a tournament before the king. The Protector used this coat and crest, with the motto—*Pax quaeritur bello.*

The Cromwells as a family were prolific and long-lived. The Protector's mother died, says Thurloe, at the age of ninety-four, but more probably in her ninetieth year. She had eleven children, the youngest born when she was, at least, in her forty-sixth year. Oliver was born, at earliest, in her thirty-fifth year. Oliver himself had nine children, and thirty grandchildren, of whom at least one lived into the reign of George II. and the ministry of Walpole. Sir Henry Cromwell, the Protector's grandfather, had eleven children, the eldest of whom, Sir Oliver, died in his ninety- third year, also having had eleven children. Elizabeth, the mother of John Hampden, died at the age of ninety. Of Sir Henry Cromwell fifty-two grandchildren are recorded. During the Civil Wars there were no less than six contemporary Oliver Cromwells, all closely related. The "cousinry" of Oliver the Protector is thus an infinite field, for it ramifies into the families of the Hampdens, Barringtons, Whalleys, Trevors, St. Johns, Waltons, Dunches, Everards, Ingoldsbys, Gerards; and includes the families of Earl of Buckinghamshire, Lord Dacre, Lord Hampden, and many more.

Appendix B

All the portraits of Cromwell appear to be derived from works by Coopèr, Walker, Lely, or Faithorne. Their paintings and drawings, with the medals, seem to be the only portraits taken from life. And a mask was taken after death.

Of them all the best is perhaps the large drawing by Cooper, in the house of the master, at Sidney Sussex College, Cambridge. Cooper's miniatures are very numerous and are well known—they seem to have been preferred by the Cromwell family. Evelyn thought the picture by Walker, with the page tying his scarf, so well engraved by Lombart, to be the most striking likeness. There is one main difference in the portraits. Cooper and Lely, whose portraits exactly resemble each other, paint the brows as knit, and somewhat drawn downwards. Walker and Faithorne make the brow high and well arched over the eye. So too does Simon in his medals. Perhaps the bony structure of the forehead was so formed; and the fleshy and movable eyebrows fell down when the face was seen in repose.

The following is an exact description of the features made after careful study of many portraits:

> *Eyes:* steely blue, keen, penetrating, very sad.
>
> *Forehead:* very broad, much lined, receding towards the top, nearly in a line with the nose, very prominent fleshy brow, with "the bar of Michael Angelo"—wart over right brow.
>
> *Hair:* light brown, worn in long curls, early turned ashen-gray; very slight, scanty moustache, and tuft on under lip.
>
> *Chin:* square, solid, but rather receding, fleshy.
>
> *Nose:* very thick, heavy, prominent, red.
>
> *Lips:* large, prominent, fleshy, very firmly drawn.
>
> *Complexion:* weather-beaten, coarse, fair and florid.
>
> *General Characteristics:* energetic, resolute, rough, sympathetic, melancholy, passionate.

Of the embalmed head fixed in the halberd-point in the possession of Mr. Horace Wilkinson no certain history can be given. Some competent judges have, on physical grounds, believed it to be genuine; and it does not seem to disagree with any single feature in the authentic portraits. It is not a skull, but a head, which has been thoroughly embalmed; severed, after embalming, from the body; encrusted into an ancient spear-point. It is said to have been secured by a descendant of the Protector from the soldier who was on guard when it fell from the gateway at Westminster Hall, as described by Pepys. But it adds nothing fresh to our knowledge; and from the nature of the case, it could give us no help in recalling the likeness. The Cromwellian portraits and relics, genuine and spurious, are altogether infinite, and even about the genuine alone a volume might be written.

CHAPTER III

PREPARATION FOR CIVIL WAR

A.D. 1628–1642. AETAT. 29–43

In March 1625 Charles I. began his reign amid joy and hope in the nation. In May he was married to Henrietta Maria, daughter of Henry IV. and sister of Louis XIII., King of France. Villiers, Duke of Buckingham, was the absolute ruler of the King of England, as was Richelieu of the King of France. In June Charles met his first Parliament; and the great struggle began between personal Monarchy and Parliamentary government—a struggle which continued, in a form more or less acute, for nearly one hundred years.

Charles, narrow, obstinate, and imperious, was without that Scotch canniness and turn for compromise which had saved his father in his worst hours. Villiers, equally headstrong and incapable, exaggerated all that in the previous reign had been disastrous and unpopular. The Parliament which met the new king was stronger and more conscious of its strength than any which had preceded it; and in Eliot, Pym, Wentworth, Hampden, Selden, Coke, it possessed men of real power and immense resource. From the first, it refused supplies to assist the projects of Buckingham, and it made the voting of the necessary expenses of government conditional on its own control over the entire administration of the nation, civil and religious. Directly it attacked Buckingham, after a session of less than two months it was summarily dissolved.

But Charles, overwhelmed by his liabilities and disasters abroad, was forced by his want of money to summon a new Parliament. It met in 1626, only to show a yet more determined resolve to secure ministerial responsibility as the condition of voting supplies. It formally impeached Buckingham; and after a stormy session of three months, was dissolved even more summarily than the last.

For some two years Charles and Buckingham struggled on, raising money as they could by forced loans, by arbitrary arrest, and irregular impositions; sinking from one disaster to another, until the government of the country was reduced to complete disorganisation. The miserable expeditions to Cadiz, to Rhé, the abandonment of the Huguenots of La Rochelle, the failure of all the foreign schemes and illegal exactions at home, drove the nation to the last point of exasperation. All other means of raising money failing, Charles at last consented to summon a third Parliament in 1628. It met on 17th March. It was in this third Parliament of Charles that Oliver Cromwell first entered on public life as member for Huntingdon.

It was one of the most remarkable Parliaments in our history. Those who had opposed the Court, and those who had been imprisoned, were eagerly returned. Pym, Eliot, Wentworth, Hampden, Selden, Coke, and many others of fame in the great struggle were members.

When the House met, its first act was to form a series of committees on Religion, Justice, Grievances, and Trade. It proceeded to deal with the entire range of public affairs, civil and religious, legislative and executive alike. Wentworth, at first its leading spirit, shrank back from the prospect of a real Parliamentary executive, and the lead passed to Eliot and Pym. The Petition of Right was passed—the second great title-deed of popular government. On the 10th March 1629 the House was dissolved, after two stormy sessions of less than five months in all, having taken a memorable step in the great contest—the substitution of Parliamentary for Monarchic government in England.

The substitution of Parliamentary for Personal government in England proved to be a long and singularly complex undertaking. It was not at all secured until the settlement of 1688, and it was not absolutely accepted and developed until the accession of the House of Hanover. But in 1628 the full meaning of the change was imagined by few, and the practical solution of its problems had not crossed the mind of any. None of the conditions, none of the institutions of Parliamentary government, as we now understand it, existed. No one of the greater nations of Europe had attempted anything like it; and, indeed, down to our day, no one of them has organised it into a system. In 1629 the only type of government known to the larger states of Europe was a Personal government directly controlled by an hereditary sovereign, under more or less definite limits, and with more or less representative control as to legislation and taxation. The early Parliaments of Charles did honestly believe that they were maintaining the ancient privileges of Englishmen and the old rights of the Commons of England. In reality they were doing something very different, and from the first they laid claim to a wholly greater part. They virtually claimed the real sovereignty in all things civil and religious, legislative and executive. They asserted a right to judge, punish, and control almost anything done or spoken in Church or in State; to enforce absolute conformity to a given standard in worship, opinion, and conduct; and, whilst criticising, practically to direct the entire executive authority, military, civil, ecclesiastical, and judicial.

Accustomed as we are to Parliamentary government, we are wont to forget that in the reign of Charles it was impracticable, even if it could be conceived of as an organised system. The vast majority of the nation, and at least three-fourths of the Parliament, knew of no other executive authority than that of the king's majesty, and no other ecclesiastical authority but that of the King and Church. No man had conceived of a king who reigned but did not govern, though many dreamed of a church without rulers. There were no such ideas as that of publicity in administration, as that of an executive responsible for its daily work to Parliament. There was no conception of a ministry sitting in Parliament, doing its ordinary work under the eye of Parliament, and with the help and supervision of Parliament. There was no thought yet of a Cabinet virtually nominated by the majority of the House of Commons, and unable to survive a single adverse vote. Yet without all this Parliamentary government could not exist. And Parliamentary government in this form had not crossed even the lofty and enthusiastic visions of Sir John Eliot.

The part which Cromwell took in this memorable Parliament was a very humble one. He was not thirty when it was dissolved; but on taking his seat as a young man he found himself amongst friends and relations. John Hampden, then thirty-four, was his first cousin and close friend. Sir Francis Barrington was his uncle by marriage. Sir William Masham of Otes, a neighbour of Sir J. Bourchier in Essex, who married Barrington's daughter, was Oliver's friend through life. And these men were amongst the leaders of the Puritan gentry. But the young member for Huntingdon sat and voted in silence. Once only does he seem to have taken a part in the debates. On 11th February the Committee for Religion, John Pym being in the chair, was discussing the offences of the Bishop of Winchester and others who had supported preachers condemned by the House. Cromwell rose and said that he had heard from Dr. Beard how, when a certain Dr. Alabaster had preached flat popery at Paul's Cross, the Bishop of Winchester, his diocesan, had commanded Dr. Beard to preach nothing to the contrary, and, when he persisted in so preaching, had reprimanded him. The remark was well received by the committee, and the House ordered Dr. Beard to be sent for as a witness, and the summons to be delivered to Mr. Cromwell. By the 24th of February the Resolutions on Religion were ready, but the immediate dissolution of the House put an end to debates. For more than eleven years no Parliament was called.

During these eleven years (1629-40) Cromwell lived quietly amongst his own people, and we may conveniently here set down the simple annals of his private life. His uncle Richard—godfather, we assume, to the young Richard—died in 1628, and left to Oliver a piece of land in Huntingdon, and nineteen acres of arable land near; but Cromwell was soon to quit Huntingdon for ever. In 1630 a new charter was granted to the borough, and Cromwell, Dr. Beard, and Robert Barnard were named as the justices of the peace. By the new charter the rule of the town was handed over to a mayor, and twelve aldermen appointed for life. The new charter was apparently a triumph for the king's men, and it abolished the old popular election. Cromwell was not slow or measured in remonstrating against the powers it conferred. A complaint was made by petition of the mayor and aldermen against "the disgraceful and unseemly speeches used to" the mayor and Robert Barnard. A warrant was issued, and Cromwell was brought before the Privy Council in November 1630. The affair was committed to the arbitration of the Earl of Manchester, and ended with an apology and a compromise, the charter being amended in three. points. Cromwell acknowledged that "he had spoken in heat and passion."

Huntingdon was no longer a place to hold him. In 1631 we find him paying a fine of £10 as compensation for refusing to appear at the king's coronation to be knighted. A few weeks after the award, in May 1631, Cromwell disposed of most of his property there, his mother, his wife, and his uncle Sir Oliver, joining in the deed of sale. He sold the "Augustine Fryers," the house in which he was born, with other houses, and seven acres of land in Huntingdon, and the tithes at Hartford. The sale produced £1800. Hinchinbrook had been sold four years before for £3000. He did not sell the property which came to him from his uncle Richard. With the proceeds he rented some grazing lands at St. Ives, five miles farther down the river—part of the Slepe Hall estate—and here he lived with his family for five years more until 1636. His mother and his unmarried sisters continued to live at Huntingdon, where Oliver's children were baptized down to 1637, and where he still apparently remained a proprietor. Of his life at St. Ives we know nothing. He was naturally occupied in farming; and we fancy it was in the marshy lands there that he contracted his tendency to ague. "He came to church," rumour said, "with a piece of red flannel round his neck, being subject to inflammation." And it was doubtless in these gloomy years that the "phansies" and the "melancholy" pressed most hardly on his spirit.

In January 1636 Sir Thomas Steward, his mother's brother, died; and thereon, by his uncle's will, and the settlement of his grandfather, William Steward, Cromwell became entitled to considerable property in Ely, said to be worth from £400 to £500 a year, the family house in Ely, and the goodwill to the farming of the tithes under the chapter. To Ely he removed in the course of the year 1636, living in the house still standing next to St. Mary's Church; and here his family remained until their removal to London about 1647. He at once obtained renewal of the leases held by Sir Thomas, and appears from time to time as an active trustee of the local charities and funds.

At Ely, as at St. Ives, we find him actively maintaining the Puritan preachers, and the cause of the poor. It is from St. Ives, in 1636, that he writes to Mr. Story in London to maintain a lecturer in his county—"they that procure spiritual food, they that build up spiritual temples, they are the men truly charitable, truly pious." It is from Ely, in 1638, that he writes that interesting letter to his cousin, Mrs. St. John. And in Ely, in that year, we find the little note—"Mr. Hand, I doubt not but I shall be as good as my word for your money. I desire you to deliver forty shillings of the town money to this bearer to pay for the physic for Benson's cure. [Benson was an old invalid.] If the gentlemen will not allow it at the time of account, keep this note, and I will pay it out of my own purse."

It was in these years, 1635-38, that the struggle went on about the payment of ship-money. With this he was closely connected. His cousin and friend John Hampden bore the brunt of the contest; his cousin by marriage, Oliver St. John, was Hampden's advocate in the case. Cromwell himself is reported to have also refused to pay, though, perhaps, like so many others, his case was not pressed. About the same time also took place the struggle between the poor people of the fens and the "adventurers" who had reclaimed the Bedford Level. The memoirs tell us that Cromwell took active part with the commoners. If he did so, it was not against the king, but rather against the Earl of Bedford. But we are told that as head of the discontented faction he made himself so well known that Hampden in Parliament afterwards described him "as an active person, and one that would sit well at the mark." With or without reference to this particular incident, in the Long Parliament he bore the nickname of "Lord of the Fens."

The picturesque story that he was about in these years to emigrate to America, and was stopped by an Order in Council, is without any adequate foundation. No emigrants were stopped for more than a few days. Cromwell, like Hampden, at the time was busy with important projects. And it is utterly improbable that they and the leaders of the Commons in their struggle were all about to embark in the same ship, and to abandon their cause together. But the times were gloomy and terrible to men of less nerve and energy.

These eleven years between the Parliaments of 1629 and 1640 had been times of trial. Sir John Eliot and eight members were thrown into the Tower, where in three years

Eliot died, the proto-martyr of Parliaments. Wentworth, disgusted with the pretensions of Parliament, passed over to the king; and was soon to become, with Laud, the mainstay of Personal monarchy, by whose means "Thorough" ruled for a season in State and Church. The Star Chamber prosecutions, the ferocious sentences on Prynne, Burton, Bastwick, and Lilburne, illegal fines, arbitrary taxes, the ship-money, followed. Next came the Scotch insurrection and the Covenant of 1638. The Scotch war drove Charles at last to the concession which for eleven years he had resisted. Wentworth, now Earl of Strafford, was summoned from Ireland, and he counselled a Parliament.

It met 13th April 1640; and here Oliver Cromwell was returned as member for Cambridge. The House had hardly assembled when, under the leadership of Pym, instead of voting supplies, it attacked the policy of the king in Church and State. Cromwell's name does not appear in its proceedings. The king dissolved it in anger on the 5th of May. And thus the Short Parliament, the fourth which Charles had called, was abruptly dismissed after a session of twenty-three days. But a fresh war in Scotland compelled the king within six months to summon a new House.

Everywhere the Court struggled in vain to affect the returns. The efforts of the Lord Keeper were directed to induce the electors of Cambridge to choose his own brother in place of Cromwell. But Cromwell was returned with one of the common council, in place of his former colleague, a courtier. On the 3rd of November 1640 Oliver Cromwell took his seat in the fifth Parliament of King Charles, the famous Long Parliament, which lasted for thirteen years, till dismissed by himself in 1653.

This is not the place to tell the story of the most memorable of all English Parliaments. Our concern is with Cromwell. He was now forty-one; he was already a leader amongst Puritans; and he was in close relation with prominent men in the Commons. Hampden, St. John, Henry Marten, Sir

Thomas Barrington, Sir William Masham, Valentine Walton, Edmund Waller, were his connections by marriage. To Pym, the leader of the House, to Vane, Falkland, Hyde, Holles, and Strode, he was well known as an old member. He is no longer the silent observer that he had been in 1628. From the first he takes an active part; sits on many important committees; moves several important bills. But he is in no sense a Parliamentary leader; there is no record of his making a sustained speech; nor does he appear as the chief of a distinct party. His voice was not heard during the great impeachments, or in the great political debates. His activity is confined almost. entirely to matters of religion and the oppression of persons. He is a man of influence, of suggestions, of business experience; but he nowhere appears as the orator, the tactician, or the far-sighted statesman. He does not sit with Pym and the great lawyers, but on the right of the Speaker, near Hyde and Falkland, Strode and Pennington. So far as he acts with any section it is rather with Pennington, Puritan member for the city, with Vane, Strode, and Henry Marten, the "root-and- branch" men. He abstains strictly from all debates where law, precedent, tactics are essential. His sole concern is misgovernment, corruption, and conscience.

On the third day of the session, after Pym and Hampden had uttered their great indictment of the Government, Cromwell presented the petition of John Lilburne, who had been cruelly punished by the Star-Chamber. He was appointed on the committee to consider the cases of Leighton, Prynne, Burton, Bastwick, and other victims of Laud. It was then that we have the notice of Sir Philip Warwick, already cited: "He aggravated the imprisonment of this man by the council-table unto that height that one would believe the very Government itself had been in great danger by it. I sincerely profess it lessened much my reverence unto that great council, for he was very much hearkened unto."

Within the first ten months of the Long Parliament

Cromwell was specially appointed to eighteen committees, besides those on which he sat as representing Cambridge. The most important matters came before several of those committees, and the cases of most of the sufferers from the Star-Chamber. There was another case of alleged oppression referred to one of these committees, of which Hyde, the Chancellor, has given us his own version. Lord Manchester had a dispute with some commoners of Huntingdon about a recent enclosure, which resulted in a riot, and writs were issued. Cromwell vehemently urged the case of the poor inhabitants; it was referred to a committee of which Hyde was chairman. Lord Clarendon relates that Cromwell enlarged on the evidence "with great passion"; that "in great fury" he reproached the chairman with being partial, that he bullied the witnesses, and attacked Lord Mandeville with indecency and rudeness. In the end his whole carriage was so tempestuous, and his behaviour so insolent, that the chairman was obliged to reprehend him: which Cromwell never forgave. How far all this is exaggeration we cannot now say. Cromwell and Lord Mandeville were intimate friends. And Clarendon's memory was notoriously defective, especially in all that related to himself and his opponents.

There are three great occasions where we find Cromwell in the front. Within a few weeks of the opening of Parliament, Alderman Pennington presented a petition signed by 15,000 citizens of London, calling for the abolition of Episcopacy, with all its *roots and branches*. When the debate on it came on, Pennington justified the petition, and said that he could have had fifteen times 15,000 signatures, and Cromwell eagerly intervened in the debate. He was himself interrupted with loud calls "to the bar." But, Pym and Holles supporting him, he insisted on his argument; which was "that he was more convinced of the irregularity of bishops than even before, because, like the Roman hierarchy, they would not endure to have their condition come to a trial." The matter ended for the moment in a compromise. But here, in Episcopacy, was sounded the critical note, which ultimately rallied to the king so large a portion of the people and the gentry. From that hour the king represented the Church.

The second occasion is when, on 30th December 1640, Cromwell moved the second reading of Strode's Bill for Annual Parliaments. It was referred to a select committee, on which sat Cromwell, Pym, Hampden, Strode, St. John, Holles, Selden, Barrington, Whitelocke, and others. The Bill was extremely defective from a constitutional point of view; but it ultimately took shape as the Triennial Act, one of the most important statutes of the Long Parliament. And the cardinal principle of the Annual Bill was ultimately embodied in the Bill of Rights.

The third great occasion where we find Cromwell prominent is where he prepares with Vane the Bill for the Abolition of Episcopacy, the measure which finally drove Hyde into the party of the Court. It is to the downfall of Episcopacy of the Laudian type, and for the defence of Puritanism, that Cromwell is chiefly noticed as a member of Parliament. He sits on the committee on the "Bill for the Abolishing of Superstition and Idolatry"; on the committee to consider how preaching ministers may be set up and maintained. Mr. Cromwell moves "to take some course to turn the Papists out of Dublin"; and on his motion it was ordered "that sermons should be in the afternoon in all parishes in England." But for the Church of England, but for Puritanism, the Civil War would have been a short affair, even if it ever had begun. The Long Parliament was already assuming the absolute control of public worship, and that in a definitely Presbyterian spirit. Cromwell, who burned with indignation against Laud and Popery, little saw how this claim of the Commons would prove one of his own greatest difficulties as a ruler.

But though for twelve more years this Parliament continued its bills, motions, and debates, Cromwell appears in it henceforth only in urgent matters of practical kind. The Parliament as a legislature had ceased to exist. It was a committee of safety of the nation charged with the duty of forcing the king to submit. Thus at least Cromwell viewed it. His vehemence led the Commons to take up the Grand Remonstrance, which was virtually a summons to the nation to action. It was he who on 6th November 1641 carried a resolution to give the Earl of Essex power from both Houses to command upon all occasions the trained bands on that side of Trent for the defence of the kingdom, and "*that this power should continue until the Parliament should take further order.*" Here is the first suggestion of a Parliamentary army.

On 22nd November took place the final debate on the Remonstrance, which was virtually the call to arms. We know already how vehemently Cromwell threw himself into the measure. It was one of the most memorable scenes that have ever passed in the House. Wild with excitement and party fury—the majority had been but eleven—the members drew their swords; and but for the serene good sense of Hampden, they seemed likely to fight out the Civil War on the floor of the House.

When, after sixteen hours of debate, at four in the morning, they passed out, Falkland asked Cromwell (we are told by Clarendon) if there had been a debate or not. "I will take your word for it, again," said he. "If the Remonstrance had been rejected, I would have sold all I had the next morning, and never have seen England any more; and I know there are many other honest men of this same resolution." The memory of Clarendon is quite untrustworthy. But some such conversation did probably pass. The failure of the Remonstrance would have been a different thing from the tyranny of the king. It would have meant that a majority of the Commons accepted Monarchy and Church, and Cromwell may have turned his thoughts to the New World, as did Lord Brooke and others, and probably Hampden.

The news of the Irish Rebellion and massacre, enormously exaggerated as it was, reached London in November, and stimulated the passions of all. The ferment broke out in continual riots; arms were drawn on both sides; and bands of men came trooping into London. In January 1642 the king made his ill-starred attempt to seize the five members: on 10th January he left Whitehall, never to return a king. In February Cromwell offers £500 towards the service of the Commonwealth, his cousin Hampden subscribing £1000. In July blood was drawn. In the same month Cromwell sent down arms to Cambridge, expended £100 of his own in that service, and moved to raise in Cambridge two companies of volunteers. In August he seized the magazine in the Castle of Cambridge, and secured the University plate, worth £20,000, which was being sent to the king. The House passed an indemnity, and repaid the money he had expended in arming the town. Cromwell was, in fact, committed to acts of treason and war. He, who nine months before had first suggested that a Parliamentary army should be formed under Essex, who in the interval had been rousing his own constituents to arm, was the first to strike a blow in the coming combat. The Civil War had now begun. For the next nine years his life is that of a soldier.

CHAPTER IV

THE FIRST CIVIL WAR – EDGEHILL – THE EASTERN ASSOCIATION – MARSTON MOOR

A.D. 1642–1644. AETAT. 43–45

On the 22nd of August 1642, in cloud and storm, King Charles planted the royal standard on the castle rock of Nottingham, and formally opened the Civil War. He soon found himself at the head of an army of 10,000, led by men trained in the Dutch and German wars. Prince Rupert, a born *sabreur*, now just twenty-three, was made General of the Horse. Another skilled soldier, the Earl of Lindsey, was named Commander-in-Chief. But the king's army was a motley body, and he was swayed by varying counsels. Side by side stood great nobles and gallant gentlemen, who had armed their retainers and tenants, soldiers of fortune, heroic spirits like the Verneys and Falkland, reprobates like Goring, and dissolute idlers both from town and country. There was little or no regular discipline, and a constantly shifting system of command. Charles, who in war as in peace could trust no man and adopt no counsel without secret reserves and constant vacillation, listened by turns to the groups which surrounded him—skilled tacticians, fiery swordsmen, acute statesmen, intriguers, desperadoes, and lastly, his evil spirit, his beloved, dauntless, wrong-headed wife.

The army of the Parliament was soon assembled round

Northampton, where it mustered to the number of 20,000 men. Its commander was Robert Devereux, Earl of Essex, son of Elizabeth's attainted favourite, now chief of the Parliamentary nobles, a Puritan, and a soldier trained in the foreign wars. Sincere, brave, honourable, diligent, but weak and utterly dull, he mistook his great position for capacity, and never learned how incompetent he was for all but moderate undertakings. His task was indeed not slight. The Parliamentary army, though twice as numerous, was no less heterogeneous than that of the king; it was hardly more disciplined; it had fewer officers trained to war, and fewer soldiers inured to arms. Its cavalry was inferior in equipment and skill to the dashing horsemen who followed Rupert. And though a goodly proportion were earnest Puritans, full of courage and devotion, both troops of horse and regiments of foot were largely made up of mere holiday soldiers, without character, heart, or knowledge of their business. On both sides there were germs of a splendid army, but both as yet were the musters of armed citizens, with ignorance, carelessness, and ruffianism in nearly equal degrees, with some heroes and many vagabonds.

In wealth, in numbers, and in cohesion the Parliament was stronger than the king. To him there had rallied most of the greater nobles, many of the lesser gentry, some proportion of the richer citizens, the townsmen of the west, and the rural population generally of the west and north of England. For the Parliament stood a strong section of the peers and greater gentry, the great bulk of the lesser gentry, the townsmen of the richer parts of England, the whole eastern and home counties, and lastly, the city of London. But as the Civil War did not sharply divide classes, so neither did it geographically bisect England. Roughly speaking, aristocracy and peasantry, the Church, universities, the world of culture, fashion, and pleasure were loyal: the gentry, the yeomanry, trade, commerce, morality, and law inclined to the Parliament. Broadly divided, the north and west went for the king; the south and east for the Houses; but the lines of demarcation were never exact: cities, castles, and manor-houses long held out in an enemy's county. There is only one permanent limitation. Draw a line from the Wash to the Solent. East of that line the country never yielded to the king; from first to last it never failed the Parliament. Within it are enclosed Norfolk, Suffolk, Essex, Cambridge, Huntingdon, Bedford, Bucks, Herts, Middlesex, Surrey, Kent, Sussex. This was the wealthiest, the most populous, and the most advanced portion of England. With Gloucester, Reading, Bristol, Leicester, and Northampton, it formed the natural home of Puritanism.

For two years the Civil War drags on its varying course, with cruel waste in blood, treasure, and general well-being. As is usually seen with citizen armies commanded by civilian officers, bloody encounters lead to no results; one wing in a battle is in flight whilst the other is pursuing a defeated enemy; victorious armies mysteriously melt away, and independent generals fight for their own hand. Though the king had more competent leaders and more efficient troopers than the Parliament, his own caprice and presumption, and the lawless spirits around him, continually destroyed his prospects of success. On the other side, the local and temporary character of the Parliamentary levies, the want of military habits and skilled leaders, the disorganisation inherent in a civilian army, controlled by a civilian committee, led to the failure of expeditions more numerous and better found than those of the king. In spite of noble efforts and much individual heroism, the cause of the Parliament on the whole lost ground, until, after two years of fighting, it held little more than a third of the kingdom. From this imminent peril it was rescued by Marston Moor and the New Model.

It is no part of this work to narrate the incidents of the Civil War, with all its inevitable misery, waste, and failure. The business before us is the work of Oliver Cromwell.

First he is captain of a troop, like himself yeomen and farmers who had girt on the sword for conscience' sake; then colonel of a regiment; soon general of a corps of cavalry; at last leader of an army. Steadily the discipline and fervour of his troop spread to the rest; till he organises the armies of the Parliament on the "Model" of which his own troop was the germ; and ultimately he is the commander-in-chief of armies, of which he is himself the soul—armies which in discipline, valour, and perfection of all martial qualities have never been surpassed in the annals of war.

The army of the Parliament was on paper about 20,000 foot and 5,000 horse, there being twenty regiments of infantry and seventy-five troops of horse, each troop counting sixty sabres, raised and equipped by its own captain. Oliver Cromwell was captain of the 67th troop, with his brother-in-law, John Desborough, as quartermaster. His eldest son Oliver was cornet in the 8th troop; his future son-in-law, Henry Ireton, was captain of the 58th troop. His cousin, John Hampden, was colonel of the 20th regiment of foot; his neighbour, Lord Mandeville, afterwards Earl of Blanchester, was colonel of the 10th. His brother-in-law, Valentine Walton, was captain of the 73rd troop, with Valentine the younger as cornet. Edward Whalley, his cousin, was cornet in the 60th troop. Cromwell was thus surrounded in the field by his relations, friends, and political colleagues. On the 13th of September he was ordered to muster his troop and to join the Earl of Essex.

The war opened as civil wars do: gallant skirmishes, inexplicable panics, ill-judged expeditions, and aimless marching to and fro. The first battle of the war revealed the strength and the weakness of both armies. Essex, as he followed Charles on the march to London, unexpectedly, and with but part of his force, came up with the king at Edgehill in Warwickshire. The battle began late in the afternoon of Sunday, the 23rd of October. Charles was superior in numbers, in artillery, in cavalry, and in position, Rupert, on the right wing, charging furiously, and, aided by treachery, routed and drove the left wing of Essex into Kineton, where, falling to plunder, he was in turn driven out by the arrival of Hampden and a strong rear-guard. The king's left wing also routed part of the right wing of Essex, who, believing the day lost, seized a pike and prepared to die on foot at the head of his regiment. But as the entire royal cavalry were pursuing and plundering far from the main battle, the day was restored to the Parliament by their horse on the right wing. Here were thirteen unbroken troops, of which one was that of Cromwell. Dashing into the royal infantry they destroyed one regiment after another; and acting with the remnants of Essex's foot, they cut to pieces the king's red guards, took his standard, killing Sir Edmund Verney, his standard-bearer, and the Earl of Lindsey, the late commander-in-chief. But two of his regiments remained on the field; and Charles, with his sons, was in imminent danger of capture.

At this moment Rupert and the cavalry, returning in confusion from pursuit and their combat with Hampden, found their army a rout, but they were still strong enough to save the remnants. Night closed the fight. About 4000 men lay on the bloody field, the loss of the king being greatest both in numbers and quality. It was a drawn battle, from which neither side reaped any gain. Its only result was to show first the radical unsteadiness of the Parliamentary army, the disorganisation of the king's command, his weakness in infantry, the recklessness of Rupert, and the splendid material in the Puritan regiments and troops. Essex, Stapylton, Lord Brooke, and Cromwell were especially mentioned as leaders "who never stirred from their troops; but they and their troops fought bravely till the last minute of the fight." It was the Puritan regiments of Essex, of Hoiles, and the troops raised in the eastern counties, which had saved a lost battle and destroyed the king's infantry.

The eye of a soldier would see in that first trial all the

perils and all the hopes of the situation. And a great soldier was there. It was about this time, probably a little before Edgehill, that there took place between Cromwell and Hampden the memorable conversation which fifteen years afterwards the Protector related in a speech to his second Parliament. It is a piece of autobiography so instructive and so pathetic that it must be set forth in full in the words of Cromwell himself:

> "I was a person who, from my first employment, was suddenly preferred and lifted up from lesser trusts to greater; from my first being a Captain of a Troop of Horse. ... I had a very worthy Friend then; and he was a very noble person, and I know his memory is very grateful to all,—Mr. John Hampden. At my first going out into this engagement, I saw our men were beaten at every hand. . . . 'Your troops,' said I, 'are most of them old decayed serving-men, and tapsters, and such kind of fellows; and,' said I, 'their troops are gentlemen's sons, younger sons and persons of quality: do you think that the spirits of such base mean fellows will ever be able to encounter gentlemen, that have honour and courage and resolution in them?' Truly I did represent to him in this manner conscientiously; and truly I did tell him: 'You must get men of a spirit: and take it not ill what I say,—I know you will not,—of a spirit that is likely to go on as far as gentlemen will go: or else you will be beaten still.' I told him so; I did truly. He was a wise and worthy person; and he did think that I talked a good notion, but an impracticable one. ... I raised such men as had the fear of God before them, as made some conscience of what they did; and from that day forward, I must say to you, they were never beaten, and wherever they were engaged against the enemy, they beat continually. And truly this is a matter of praise to God: and it hath some instruction in it, To own men who are religious and godly."

The issue of the whole war lay in that word. It lay with "such men as had some conscience in what they did." "From that day forward they were never beaten." The history of the formation of these Puritan armies is too important to be passed; and it has been described for us by contemporaries both friendly and hostile. Baxter says:

> "He has a special care to get religious men into his troop: these men were of greater understanding than common soldiers, . . . and making not money, but that which they took for the public felicity, to be their end, they were the more engaged to be valiant; as far as I could learn, they never once ran away before an enemy. Hereupon lie got a commission to take some care of the associated counties, where he brought this troop into a double regiment of fourteen full troops [840 men]; and all those as full of religious men as he could get. These having more than ordinary wit and resolution, had more than ordinary success."

Whitelocke says:

> "He had a brave regiment of horse of his countrymen, most of them freeholders and freeholders' sons, and who upon matter of conscience engaged in this quarrel, and under Cromwell. And thus being well armed within by the satisfaction of their own consciences, and without, by good iron arms, they would as one man stand firmly and charge desperately."

Cromwell, who turned out as a mere captain of yeomanry, with no more knowledge of war than the ordinary drill of the train-bands, acquired his knowledge of the soldier's art from Captain John Dalbier, a veteran of Dutch extraction, who had seen service abroad. We are told that he would diligently drill his troopers, instructing them in the handling of their weapons and the management of their horses. "As an officer," says Waller, "he was obedient, and did never dispute my orders or argue upon them."

Memorable indeed is the impression produced by these men on the imagination of their countrymen. On both sides the memoirs and journals record their iron discipline, their fiery zeal, their desperate courage:

"... Led in fight, yet leader seemed
Each warrior single as in chief, expert
When to advance, or stand, or turn the sway
Of battle, open when, and when to close
The ridges of grim war; no thought of flight,
None of retreat, no unbecoming deed
That argued fear; each on himself relied,
As only in his arm the moment lay
Of victory; deeds of eternal fame
Were done, but infinite; for wide was spread
That war and various."

"As for Colonel Cromwell," writes a news-letter of May 1643, "he hath 2000 brave men, well disciplined; no man swears but he pays his twelve-pence; if he be drunk, he is set in the stocks, or worse; if one calls the other roundhead he is cashiered: insomuch that the countries where they come leap for joy of them, and come in and join with them. How happy were it if all the forces were thus disciplined!"

These were the men who ultimately decided the war, and established the Commonwealth. On the field of Marston, Rupert gave Cromwell the name of "Ironside," and from thence this famous name passed to his troopers. There are two features in their history which we need to note. They were indeed "such men as had some conscience in their work"; but they were also much more. They were disciplined and trained soldiers. They were the only body of "regulars" on either side. The instinctive genius of Cromwell from the very first created the strong nucleus of a regular army, which at last in discipline, in skill, in valour, reached the highest perfection ever attained by soldiers either in ancient or modern times. The fervour of Cromwell is continually pressing towards the extension of this "regular" force. Through all the early disasters, this body of "Ironsides" kept the cause alive: at Marston it overwhelmed the king: so soon as, by the New Model, this system was extended to the whole army, the Civil War was at an end.

The scanty notices of Cromwell which in these first two years of war have come down to us give us a wonderful picture of energy, zeal, and resource. He provides for everything, goes everywhere, and wherever he comes the cause prospers, the enemy recoil. His passion stirs whole counties; his swift strokes frustrate the royalist plans; at every crisis his presence of mind improvises the one thing needful. Before the royal standard was raised, he had established patrols round Huntingdon, who watched all communication between the capital and the king at York. His first task was the organisation of a strong confederacy to block any Royalist union north with south. On the day before the battle of Edgehill the House had approved the formation of county unions for organisation and defence. Cambridge, grouping round her Norfolk, Suffolk, Essex, and Hertfordshire, formed the Eastern Association. Soon Huntingdon, and ultimately Lincoln, were added. This famous Eastern Association, strategically, was the *Torres Vedras* lines of the early Civil War—morally it became the backbone of the Parliamentary cause. "Here," says Sir Philip Warwick, "was the root of the Independency." Its founder and its soul was Cromwell. The growth of it contributed to fill up the ranks of his troops, as the formation of his regiment consolidated the Union itself. He is first named "Colonel" on 2nd March 1613. We catch gleams of him from time to time searching the houses of the disaffected, dispersing Royalist combinations, seizing plate, and unearthing conspiracies. It is in these days that he writes his famous warning to Mr. Barnard of Huntingdon: "I know you have been wary in your carriages: be not too confident thereof. Subtlety may deceive you; integrity never will." It is in these days, doubtless, that the scene took place between Oliver and his uncle, Sir Oliver, at Ramsey. "He visited him," Sir Oliver told Sir P. Warwick, "with a good strong party of horse, and asked him for his blessing, and the few hours he was there, he would not keep on his hat in his presence; but at the same time he not only disarmed but plundered him: for he took away all his plate."

In the meantime the king's cause is prospering in the north and the west. Essex lay inert, like a man who both feared defeat and did not wish for victory. Newcastle secured the north to the king, and shut up the Fairfaxes in Hull. Rupert on the west, Camden and other chiefs in the North Midlands, were raiding, plundering, and exacting contributions. It was plainly essential to gain the line of the Trent, secure Lincoln, and take Newark, the key of the Midlands. All combination to take Newark failed, in spite of Cromwell's appeals and remonstrances; but he himself advanced into Lincolnshire, occupying Peterborough, and taking Crowland. On the 13th of May he fought and won the first fight where he was in chief command. Some two miles from Grantham he met a body of Newark cavaliers who had hitherto swept the country round at their pleasure.

> "God hath given us this evening," he writes, "a glorious victory over our enemies. They were, as we are informed, one and twenty columns of horse-troops, and three or four of dragoons. It was late in the evening when we drew out; they came and faced us within two miles of the town. So soon as we had the alarm we drew out our forces, consisting of about twelve troops,—whereof some of them so poor and broken, that you shall seldom see worse: with this handful it pleased God to cast the scale; . . . and our men charging fiercely upon them, by God's providence they were immediately routed, and ran all away, and we had the execution of them two or three miles."

For the first time a body of Puritan troopers, meeting in fair onset double their number of cavaliers flushed with a victorious career, "immediately routed" them and cut them to pieces. Cromwell's men had been in arms barely nine months; but they were already formed cavalry. Their commander could not but feel that with such men ultimate victory was certain.

Elsewhere the cause of the Parliament waned. Hampden

died in June, murmuring, "Save my bleeding country;" Waller had been annihilated in the west; Bristol was taken by Rupert; and everywhere surrender to the king seemed imminent. In these straits a new effort was made to recover Lincolnshire. Cromwell took Burghley House by desperate fighting, and clearing Stamford pushed on to relieve Gainsborough. On the 28th of July, after a forced march of fifty-five miles, he met a great body of the enemy's horse, under Cavendish, Newcastle's kinsman, posted on a hill, two miles from Gainsborough.

> "We came up," he says, "horse to horse; where we disputed it with our swords and pistols a pretty time; all keeping close order, so that one could not break through the other. At last, they a little shrinking, our men perceiving it pressed in upon them, and immediately routed this whole body; some flying on the one side and others on the other of the enemy's reserve; and our men, pursuing them, had chase and execution about five or six miles."

But Cromwell was no ungovernable Rupert. Looking round he saw one regiment of the enemy's reserve still unbroken, and preparing to fall on his own rear. Rallying his men, he charged the Royalist general unawares, forced him down the hill into a quagmire, and cut his regiment to pieces, and killed young Cavendish. "My captain-lieutenant," wrote Cromwell, "slew him with a thrust under his short ribs. The rest of the body was wholly routed, not one man staying upon the place."

Gainsborough was relieved and supplied; but the day was not over. A fresh enemy was descried on the other side of the town. They too were thrust back; till presently the scanty forces of the Parliament found themselves face to face with the main army of Newcastle. The peril was extreme.; the footmen from Gainsborough were driven in; but Cromwell divided his troops into two parties, caused them to retreat in turns, facing the enemy's fresh horse; and at length, by nine removes, he drew off his whole command, all exhausted as it was, from before Newcastle's army, with the loss of only two men. For the second time Cromwell's troopers had utterly routed the cavalier squadrons in a fair charge. But this last combat proved much more. It had shown, in one of the most difficult operations in war (a small body of horse holding an army in check, whilst its own infantry retreats), unfaltering discipline in the men and masterly tactics in their handling. This affair is the first glimpse we obtain of really scientific war. The Ironsides were now led by a consummate general of horse. "This," wrote Whitelocke, "was the beginning of his Great fortunes, and he now began to appear in the world."

Before Newcastle's northern army Cromwell could do nothing but retreat. On the third day he was at Huntingdon, eighty miles away. His appeals to the committee become desperate.

> "If I could speak words to pierce your hearts," he writes, "with the sense of our and your condition, I would! . . . If somewhat be not done in this, you will see Newcastle's army march up into your bowels" (31st July). "It's no longer disputing, but out instantly all you can! Raise all your bands; send them to Huntingdon;—get up what volunteers you can; hasten your horses. Send these letters to Norfolk, Suffolk, and Essex, without delay. I beseech you spare not, but be expeditious and industrious! Almost all our foot have quitted Stamford: there is nothing to interrupt an enemy, but our horse, that is considerable. You must act lively; do it without distraction. Neglect no means" (6th August). "I beseech you hasten your levies, what you can; especially those of foot! Quicken all our friends with new letters upon this occasion. . . . Gentlemen, make them able to live and subsist that are willing to spend their blood for you" (8th August).

If Cromwell's thin line of troopers had been broken by Newcastle in that month of August, London would have been open, and the issue of the war might have changed.

The day after the last of these letters, 9th August, the House resolved to raise the infantry of the Association to 10,000, and to appoint the Earl of Manchester as Major-General. Cromwell was one of his four colonels of horse, and soon became second in command. All this time, as during the months preceding, he is beating up recruits, imploring money, and organising his troops.

> "Lay not too much upon the back of a poor gentleman, who desires, without much noise, to lay down his life and bleed the last drop to serve the cause and you" (28th May). "I advise you that your 'foot company' may be turned into a troop of horse; which indeed will, by God's blessing, far more advantage the cause than two or three companies of foot: especially if your men be honest godly men, which by all means I desire" (2nd August). "Hasten your horses;—a few hours may undo you, neglected. I beseech you be careful what captains of horse you choose, what men be mounted: a few honest men are better than numbers. Some time they must have for exercise. If you choose godly honest men to be captains of horse, honest men will follow them; and they will be careful to mount such. ... I had rather have a plain russet-coated captain that knows what he fights for, and loves what lie knows, than that which you call 'a gentleman' and is nothing else. I honour a gentleman that is so indeed!"

To Oliver St. John he writes (11th September):

> "My troops increase. I have a lovely company; you would respect them, did you know them. They are no 'Anabaptists'; they are honest sober Christians:—They expect to be used as Men! . . . I desire not to seek myself:—'but' I have little money of my own to help my Soldiers. My estate is little. I tell you, the business of Ireland and England hath had of me, in money, between Eleven and Twelve Hundred pounds;—therefore my Private can do little to help the Public. You have had my money: I hope in God I desire to venture my skin. So do mine. Lay weight upon their patience; but break it not!"

Cromwell's spirit, rousing Association and Parliament, together with the inherent rottenness in the king's forces, averted the immediate danger. In September the House took the Solemn League and Covenant, the Presbyterian charter, as the condition of obtaining an army from Scotland. The Fairfaxes held out gallantly at Hull, and a combined movement of three forces, under Manchester, Willoughby, and Cromwell, pushed steadily into Lincolnshire. On 22nd September Cromwell relieved and entered Hull, where began his brotherhood-in-arms with Fairfax. He brought Sir Thomas and his horse into Lincoln. On 11th October the combined horse met near Winceby a strong force of cavalry from Newark. The numbers were nearly equal, some three thousand troopers on either side. Cromwell's men were worn out with their marches, and he would have declined a combat could it have been done. At the sight of the enemy the spirit of his troopers rose, and they charged, singing psalms, Cromwell leading the van, assisted by Manchester and seconded by Fairfax. He "fell with brave resolution upon the enemy"; his horse was killed under him at the first charge and fell down upon him; as he rose up, he was knocked down again by the gentleman who charged him. He seized a trooper's horse and mounted himself again, and prepared to head a second charge. "The enemy stood not another; but were driven back upon their own body, which was to have seconded them; and at last put these into a plain disorder; and thus in less than half an hour's fight they were all quite routed." The enemy were chased, slaughtered, drowned, and dispersed; a scanty remnant reached Newark. Thus a third time Cromwell's horse had in fair fight scattered the cavalier cavalry like chaff. On the following day Newcastle abandoned the siege of Hull; on the 20th of the same month Manchester took Lincoln. From that date Lincolnshire passed to the cause of the Parliament, and the result of the campaign was to win for it the whole east of England, as far north as the Humber.

The year 1644 opened with better prospects for the Parliament. In January a Scotch army of 20,000 men came to their assistance; Cromwell, reappearing in the House, charged Lord Willoughby with misconduct, and induced it to name Manchester to the sole command in the seven associated counties; and in February it appointed the Committee of Both Kingdoms the supreme executive authority for the conduct of the war. Cromwell, Manchester, St. John, and the Vanes were named members of it. Manchester made Cromwell his lieutenant-general. A contemporary tells us that "Manchester himself, a quiet, meek man, permitted his lieutenant-general, Cromwell, to guide all the army at his pleasure. The man is a very wise and active head, universally well beloved, as religious as stout. Being a known Independent, the most of the soldiers, who loved new ways, put themselves under his command." The situation therefore was this. The whole of Eastern England, from the Humber to the Thames, was firmly organised under one command, which was practically that of Cromwell. This army was composed almost wholly of zealous Puritans. And Cromwell, its real chief, was the ruling member of the Committee of the Association, and at the same time a member of the Committee of Both Kingdoms.

No sooner was the Covenant taken by Parliament than it was resolved to force its acceptance on the Associated Counties at least. Cromwell was Governor of Ely, and Manchester was ordered to impose the Covenant on Cambridge. This was carried out in its stern severity by both; and the ritual of the Church was forcibly suppressed, and the ancient art symbolism ruthlessly destroyed. It was then that took place the destruction of statues, carvings and glass, the harrying of divines, and the scene in Ely Cathedral, with Mr. Hitch. Cromwell had by letter peremptorily ordered this clergyman "to forbear altogether his choir-service, so unedifying and offensive." Mr. Hitch persisting in it, Cromwell with his guard marched into the church, with his hat on, we are told (he was on actual military duty); he called out, "I am a man under authority, and am commanded to dismiss this assembly." Mr. Hitch still persevered with his service; whereupon Cromwell broke out, "Leave off your fooling and come down, sir!": which he did. The ring of the "sharp untuneable voice" is not pleasant here; nor is driving a priest from his pulpit an honourable mission. Cromwell had in him a strong vein of coarseness: he was a soldier in a civil war executing peremptory orders, and neither he nor any Puritan of that age would ever allow that terms could be kept with Popish or semi-Popish divines.

Though Cromwell could not rise superior to his age where Romish ritual was concerned, he was far above his Presbyterian comrades in true toleration. The exigencies of war and government broadened his view of religion, till he ultimately rose to be the most tolerant statesman of his time. Even now, amidst these vile tasks of wrecking cathedrals and ejecting priests, we can see his native spirit asserting its freedom. Major-General Crawford, a zealous Scotch Presbyterian, Cromwell's rival and secret enemy, had suspended and arrested a certain colonel. Cromwell writes sharply to Crawford:

> "Surely you are not well advised thus to turn off one so faithful to the cause, and so able to serve you as this man is. Give me leave to tell you I cannot be of your judgment; if a man notorious for wickedness, for oaths, for drinking, hath as great a share in your affection as one who fears an oath, who fears to sin. . . . Ay, but the man 'is an Anabaptist.' Are you sure of that? Admit he be, shall that render him incapable to serve the public? 'He is indiscreet.' It may be so, in some things: we have all human infirmities. . . . *Sir, the State, in choosing men to serve it, takes no notice of their opinions*; if they be willing faithfully to serve it,—that satisfies. I advised you formerly to bear with men of different minds from yourself: if you had done it when I advised you to it, I think you would not have had so many stumbling-blocks in your way. . . . Take heed of being sharp, or

> too easily sharpened by others against those to whom you can object little but that they square not with you in every opinion concerning matters of religion."

This is the first open avowal of Cromwell's attitude. He was opposed root and branch to Presbyterianism as a narrow and oppressive formalism; and he long delayed to sign the Covenant. He was an Independent, and the chief of the Independents. About doctrines and forms of worship he cared little. Bible religion, as understood by Puritans, was the one thing needful; subject to that, freedom of conscience to all forms of worship. Papists were enemies of the common weal: the ministers of a State Church should not practise Popish rites. Vice, profanity, slackness were not to be borne in the ranks. But every zealous, moral, God-fearing servant of the State should be free to follow his own conscience.

All through the spring we find Cromwell active on various services in the counties of Bucks, Warwick, Oxford, Cambridge, and Lincoln. He took Hillesden House, Banbury, and secured Sleaford. The whole country east of the Trent and the upper Thames was now nearly recovered to the Parliament. In the west all was confusion and failure. But the long-planned deliverance of the north was at length at hand. In April the Scots joined Manchester and the Fairfaxes before York; and by the end of June the combined forces numbered about 24,000 men, under Leven, Fairfax, and Manchester. At Marston Moor, eight miles from York, on the 2nd July, they met a combined army of nearly equal strength under Rupert, Newcastle, and Goring.

The day was dull and thunderous, with occasional showers; and it was far into the afternoon before the two armies were in position. Hour after hour they stood on the moor glaring at each other across the ditch which parted them; each watching for his opportunity to attack. The Parliament's men occupied a slight hill, and stood to arms in the long corn, from time to time chanting a psalm. Rupert had advanced his men to the front for immediate attack; but the older generals of the king induced him to defer the combat. A desultory cannonade began on both sides, and here Cromwell's nephew, young Valentine Walton, lost his life. The armies were thus drawn up—Cromwell commanded the left wing, where he had, besides the infantry of the Eastern Association, some 4200 horsemen, directly fronting Rupert and his cavaliers. Nine thousand Scotch infantry held the centre, opposed to Newcastle and the main body of the Royalists. The two Fairfaxes led the right wing, facing Goring and his cavalry. It was seven o'clock in the summer afternoon—the royal generals had retired for repose—when the army of the Parliament suddenly fell on Rupert. Horse and foot of the Eastern Association were at once across the ditch in one headlong charge. Cromwell in person dashed into Rupert's chosen regiment. He was slightly wounded in the neck by a shot. "Amiss is as good as a mile," he cried; and the flower of the cavalry in both armies were locked in a deadly grapple, "hacking one another at the sword point." For a moment the Ironsides reeled, but their reserve of three Scotch regiments pressing on behind, Cromwell speedily broke the whole Royalist chivalry, "and scattered them before him like a little dust." But as his foremost lines were chasing and slaughtering the flying cavaliers to the very gates of York, the general held in hand his main force, and paused, as he had done at Gainsborough, to see how the battle sped on his right.

It was indeed speeding ill, and was all but an utter rout. Fairfax's men on the right wing had been cut to pieces, and chased into Tadcaster by Goring's horsemen; and, dashing in wild flight into their own infantry in their rear, they had utterly broken the whole wing. Goring turned on to the flank of the Scots in the centre, whilst Newcastle's border regiment, known as the Whitecoats, assailed them in front. The Scots, fighting bravely, were all but overwhelmed. Whole regiments broke and fled, and but three remained on the field. The Earl of Leven, their commander, believing all lost, fled towards Leeds; Lord Fairfax and the Earl of Manchester were swept away for a time in the melee.

As Cromwell rallied his men from the tremendous charge which had broken Rupert like dust, a disastrous sight met his eyes. Sir Thomas Fairfax, wounded in the face, with his charger wounded, had forced his way through to the Royalist rear; but he was separated from his men, and had lost all touch with his command. From him Cromwell learned that the right wing was dispersed, and the centre in desperate straits. In this strange battle, whilst the prince, the Royalist commander-in-chief, was flying with his men miles away to the north, the three generals of the Parliament were flying with the fragments of their troops far away to the south. In an hour the genius of Cromwell had changed disaster into victory. Launching the Scotch troopers of his own wing against Newcastle's Whitecoats, and the infantry of the Eastern Association to succour the remnants of the Scots in the centre, he swooped with the bulk of his own cavalry round the rear of the king's army, and fell upon Goring's victorious troopers on the opposite side of the field. Taking them in the rear, all disordered as they were in the chase and the plunder, he utterly crushed and dispersed them. Having thus with his own squadron annihilated the cavalry of both the enemy's wings, he closed round upon the Royalist centre; and there the Whitecoats and the remnants of the king's infantry were cut to pieces almost to a man.

Such startling results, so suddenly achieved, are not very hard to explain. The armies which fought at Marston consisted, with one exception, of brave but untrained militia. On both sides the command was divided and the cohesion loose, and that in the army of the Parliament even more than in that of the king. None of the generals, except Rupert and Cromwell, had any real capacity, and Rupert was madly overweening and reckless. But the 4000 horsemen whom Cromwell led were a perfectly trained and regular corps of cavalry; as the veteran Lesley said, "Europe hath no better soldiers." Their leader was an almost ideal general of cavalry—furious in the charge, rapid in insight, wary, alert, and master of himself. There was nothing to surprise us, therefore, that a splendid corps of regular cavalry, led by a consummate tactician, should thus in an hour ride down an ill-led, ill-ordered army of militiamen.

It was a crushing and bloody overthrow. The chase and slaughter continued till ten at night. Four thousand Royalists, the flower of the king's men, lay on the field, and the white skins of the slain revealed how many of his silken courtiers had fallen. Colours, arms, supplies, baggage, and papers fell to the victors. The king's army was destroyed, and Rupert's prestige was gone. The prince and his chosen cavaliers had indeed been swept from the field "like chaff." The fugitives from the Parliament's army drew back to the ranks; and Leven and his generals learned the next day that they had won a mighty success.

In a noble letter to his sister's husband Cromwell recounted the victory, and then suddenly broke to him the news of his son's death. He writes thus on the 5th of July to Colonel Valentine Walton:

> "It's our duty to sympathise in all mercies; and to praise the Lord together in chastisements or trials, that so we may sorrow together.
>
> "Truly England and the Church of God hath had a great favour from the Lord, in this great Victory given unto us, such as the like never was since this War began. It had all the evidences of an absolute Victory obtained by the Lord's blessing upon the Godly Party principally. We never charged but we routed the enemy. The Left Wing, which I commanded, being our own horse, saving a few Scots in our rear, beat all the Prince's horse. God made them as stubble to our swords. We charged their regiments of foot with our horse, and routed all we charged. The particulars I cannot relate now; but I believe, of Twenty Thousand the Prince hath not Four Thousand left. Give glory, all the

glory, to God.

"Sir, God hath taken away your eldest Son by a cannon-shot. It break his leg. We were necessitated to have it cut off, whereof he died.

"Sir, you know my own trials this way: but the Lord supported me with this, That the Lord took him into the happiness we all pant for and live for. There is your precious child full of glory, never to know sin or sorrow any more. He was a gallant young man, exceedingly gracious. God give you His comfort. . . . Truly he was exceedingly beloved in the Army, of all that knew him. But few knew him; for he was a precious young man, tit for God. You have cause to bless the Lord. He is a glorious Saint in Heaven; wherein you ought exceedingly to rejoice. Let this drink up your sorrow; seeing these are not feigned words to comfort you, but the thing is so real and undoubted a truth. You may do all things by the strength of Christ. Seek that, and you shall easily bear your trial. Let this public mercy to the Church of God make you to forget your private sorrow. The Lord be your strength."

The immediate effect of the victory of Marston was to give the north of England to the Parliament. Rupert, rallying a force of cavaliers, broke round by the northwest into Lancashire; the other royal generals dispersed, and York, Newcastle, and other strongholds in the north fell one after another to the Parliament. Within a few months the whole north of England was practically theirs. And a line drawn from the Mersey to the Thames at London, and thence to Southampton water, would thenceforth roughly enclose the England which acknowledged the Houses.

CHAPTER V

THE NEW MODEL – NASEBY – END OF THE FIRST CIVIL WAR

A.D. 1645–1646. AETAT. 46–47

The great success at Marston, which had given the north to the Parliament, was all undone in the south and west through feebleness and jealousies in the leaders and the wretched policy that directed the war. Detached armies, consisting of a local militia, were aimlessly ordered about by a committee of civilians in London. Disaster followed on disaster. Essex, Waller, and Manchester would neither agree amongst themselves nor obey orders. Essex and Waller had parted before Marston was fought; Manchester had returned from York to protect his own eastern counties. Waller, after his defeat at Cropredy, did nothing, and naturally found his army melting away. Essex, perversely advancing into the west, was outmanoeuvred by Charles, and ended a campaign of blunders by the surrender of all his infantry.

By September 1644 throughout the whole south-west the Parliament had not an army in the field. But the committee of the Houses still toiled on with honourable spirit, and at last brought together near Newbury a united army nearly double the strength of the king's. On Sunday, the 29th of October, was fought the second battle of Newbury, as usual in these ill-ordered campaigns, late in the afternoon. An arduous day ended without victory, in spite of the greater numbers of the Parliament's army, though the men fought well, and their officers led them with skill and energy. At night the king was suffered to withdraw his army without loss, and later to carry off his guns and train. The urgent appeals of Cromwell and his officers could not infuse into Manchester energy to win the day, or spirit to pursue the retreating foe.

Such want of skill and of heart roused Cromwell to indignation. And the differences between himself and Manchester, which had long been smouldering, blazed into a flame. Cromwell was the recognised chief of the Independents, Manchester was now a leader of the Presbyterians; Cromwell was resolved to beat the king, Manchester was now eager for peace; Cromwell was the leader of the farmers and yeomen who were bent on a thorough reform, Manchester represented the great peers who already feared that rebellion had gone too far. Cromwell, in filling his regiments with zealous soldiers, refused to take account of their religions and dogmas or their social position. To him a God-fearing man, stout in the charge and orderly in his conduct, was worthy of any post, were he the son of peer or peasant. He told Manchester that such soldiers as he sought would prevent the making a dishonourable place. The rise of independency now began to alarm the rich and well-born Puritans, just as the rise of Presbyterianism had driven over to the king so many rich and well-born Churchmen. Cromwell had told Manchester that he hoped "to live to see never a nobleman in England," and that it would not be well till he was but plain Mr. Montague. Cromwell had never at any time any definite leaning towards social revolution. But the set of circumstances was forcing him to see how Crown and Peerage held together, how spiritual freedom was bound up with social change. He was even reported to have said that "if he met the king in battle, he would fire his pistol at him as at another." The time was come when those who had resolved to carry the work through were to take the place of those who had but half a heart. At a council of war, called on 10th November, Manchester said, "If we beat the king ninety and nine times, yet he is king still, and so will his posterity be after him; but if the king beat us once we shall be all hanged, and our posterity made slaves."—"My lord," replied Cromwell, "if this be so, why did we take up arms at first? This is against fighting ever hereafter. If so, let us make peace, be it never so base." Cromwell resolved to strike a great blow.

During this autumn Cromwell more than once returned to his place in Parliament; and for some months in the winter of 1644-45 we find his principal activity there. In September he had in vain attempted the removal of General Crawford, the Scotch representative of Presbyterianism in the eastern army. The campaign of Newbury decided him to attack Manchester.

On the 25th of November he exhibited in the House a formal charge against the Earl of Manchester, to the effect "That the said Earl hath always been indisposed and backward to engagements, and the ending of the war by the sword; and for such a peace as a victory would be a disadvantage to", and the charge went on to specify in detail that since the taking of York, and especially before Newbury, he had declined to take further advantage of the enemy, and on many fit opportunities to bring him to battle.

Cromwell's speech made a deep impression on the House, and a committee was appointed to consider his charge, Mr. Zouch Tate as chairman. The Earl of Manchester defended himself, and in turn charged Cromwell with insubordination. A long and ineffective dispute was carried on in both Houses. The Scotch representatives consulted some leading members if General Cromwell, the avowed enemy of Crawford, could not be proceeded against as "an incendiary." Whitelocke and Maynard told them that, without better proof, he was far too strong in both Houses to attempt it. At length Cromwell resolved on his great stroke for reorganising the army.

On the 9th of December the House was in committee to consider the sad condition of the kingdom. "There was general silence for a good space of time." At length Cromwell rose and spoke to this effect:

> "It is now a time to speak, or for ever hold the tongue. The important occasion now, is no less than To save a Nation, out of a bleeding, nay, almost dying condition: which the long continuance of this War hath already brought it into; so that without a more speedy, vigorous, and effectual prosecution of the War,—casting off all lingering proceedings like soldiers-of-fortune beyond sea, to spin out a war,—we shall make the kingdom weary of. us, and hate the name of a Parliament.
>
> "For what do the enemy say? nay, what do many say who were friends at the beginning of the Parliament? Even this, That the Members of both Houses have got great places and commands, and the sword into their hands; and, what by interest in Parliament, what by power in the Army, will perpetually continue themselves in grandeur, and not permit the War speedily to end, lest their own power should determine with it. . . .
>
> "But this I would recommend to your prudence, Not to insist upon any complaint or oversight of any Commander-in-chief upon any occasion whatsoever; for as I must acknowledge myself guilty of oversights, so I know they can rarely be avoided in military affairs. Therefore, waving a strict inquiry into the causes of these things, let us apply ourselves to the remedy; which is most necessary. And I hope we have such true English hearts, and zealous affections towards the general weal of our Mother Country, as no Members of either Houses will scruple to deny themselves, and their own private interests, for the public good; nor account it to be a dishonour done to them, whatever the Parliament shall resolve upon in this weighty matter."

Such was the first speech of Cromwell's which has come

down to us, where he appears as a statesman impressing his policy on Parliament and the nation. Both in form and in substance it is in the highest sense characteristic. There is the strong personality, the rough mother-wit, the vivid and racy phrase, as of a man in authority taking counsel with his familiars, not as of the orator addressing a senate. There is the directness of purpose with laborious care to avoid premature precision in detail, any needless opposition, and all personal offence. The form is conciliatory, guarded and qualified, almost allusive; even the specific measure recommended is left to be inferred or subsequently defined. Yet the general purpose how clear! The will behind the words how strenuous!

Thereupon Mr. Zouch Tate, in evident concert with Cromwell, proposed, "under the similitude of a boil in the thumb," what was afterwards known as the Self-denying Ordinance. By it all members of either House were required to resign their commands. Cromwell in a speech denied that this would destroy the army, which looks, he said, to the cause they fight for. Within ten days it was passed. And at a stroke the Essexes, Manchesters, the political and Presbyterian officers were removed from command.

Within two months more the New Model was passed for the army. It completely reorganised the forces of the Commonwealth. By it three irregular, disconnected armies of 10,000 each, consisting of militia and loose levies, raised for a short time, and under various authorities, were consolidated into one regular army of 22,000 horse and foot; so as to form a standing army, permanently organised under a single uniform command. Sir Thomas Fairfax was made commander-in-chief; and he busily laboured to complete its formation. The voice was the voice of Fairfax; but the hands were the hands of Oliver.

The New Model and the Self-denying Ordinance must be taken together; and together they amount to a complete revolution in the military and civil executive. By the New

Model the forces of the Parliament, hitherto the separate corps of local militia, were organised into a regular army of professional soldiers. They gained at once the cohesion, the mobility, and the discipline of a standing army. But there was much more than this in the change. The cavalry of the Eastern Association had long been a regular army in everything but name; and they formed the model for the rest. They were themselves much more than an army. They were an organised body of radical reformers, bent upon very definite objects in the spiritual and also in the civil order. And though their military discipline was rigid, they had long been permitted to carry on agitation in things religious and even political, under the specious disguise of seeking the Lord in prayer and exhortation.

Cromwell had created this singular body of Bible warriors, in the first instance, as men "who had some conscience" in the task of defeating the king, but soon deliberately, and even avowedly, as men who would stand between the Parliament and dishonourable peace. In things spiritual, they were Independent or earnest for entire liberty of conscience; in things civil, they were already tending to the Commonwealth, to political and social revolution. To organise the New Model on the frame of the Ironsides was to put the sword of the State into the hands of Independency and of radical reform.

The Independents would not have been made masters of the situation but for the Self-denying Ordinance. At a stroke it put the army into the hands of its own military chiefs; and by excluding from command members of either House, it destroyed the hold which Parliament retained over the generals. Essex and Manchester, to whom rank and wealth had given a factitious influence in a militia army, were now excluded, as was also the whole order of the peerage. Essex and Manchester represented Presbyterianism, the party of peace, and the landed gentry. To exclude them and all members of Parliament was practically to exclude these elements from command. And thus, in exchanging a force of local volunteers—the natural chiefs of which were the members of either House—for an organised army of regulars, led by professional officers, the Parliament was deliberately giving itself a master. This would have been the case had it simply created an ordinary army; but the New Model was much more than an army. It was itself a Parliament—a Parliament larger, more resolute, and far more closely knit together in spirit and will than the Parliament which continued to sit officially at Westminster. From this hour the motive power of the Revolution passed from the House of Commons to the army.

There is no reason to doubt that New Model and Self-denying Ordinance, in conception and execution, were both the work of Cromwell. The New Model was simply his own troop enlarged, as he explained it to Hampden, to Manchester, to Essex, to Crawford, in so many speeches and so many letters. The. Self-denying Ordinance was in keeping with his whole conduct in war—that of thrusting aside all but thorough-going soldiers, whose single idea was to win. As he had successively assailed Lord Willoughby, Lord Grey of Groby, Essex, Crawford, so now he got rid of Manchester, and all possible Manchesters to come. The method of carrying out the great change is equally characteristic of the man—the employment of others in the work; the energy in pushing it through with the tentative, conciliatory, and cautious way in which the details are worked out. All bears the stamp of the thorough tactician and master of men. Even now, as always later, he is not so much a Parliamentary leader as a chief having authority, who, in a formal message, is urging on the House a general policy to follow.

Did he see all the momentous bearing of the change? Did he press it in desire of personal power? Two questions the answer to which is obvious enough. Cromwell was a man whose mind was always bent on the immediate work to his hand. The urgent need of the time was an organised army of professional soldiers. Without that the king was in fair way to return in triumph. The New Model did, in fact, prove to be the saving of the cause. But Cromwell, with his keen insight, could not have been long in grasping the truth that the New Model meant not only the saving of the Parliament, but the saving of the Parliament in a certain way—utter defeat for the king, and entire liberty for conscience. Did he desire personal power? He desired the success of his cause. And he took power when it came within his grasp, in order to secure his desires. Such are the conditions of healthy statesmanship: such is the duty of a born statesman. In dealing with persons his conduct was open, moderate, and not ungenerous, even whilst most trenchant. He thrust them aside, because, whilst they remained, the work, as he cared for it, could not go on. He stepped into their place, because he knew himself fit to accomplish the work.

The New Model army was voted in January, and finally established on 19th of February 1645. Sir Thomas Fairfax was named Commander-in-Chief, with Skippon for Major-General. The second place was left open, obviously for Cromwell. There can be little doubt that the promoters of the new measure fully designed to name him. Fairfax was occupied from January to April organising the army at Windsor. It was to consist of 22,000 men—14,400 foot, 6600 horse, and 1000 dragoons. There is no evidence that Cromwell directly took part in the work. But there can be little doubt that it was done after his own heart. During these months we find him in Parliament, voting for the execution of the two traitor Hothams, and afterwards for that of Laud.

In April Cromwell was sent into the west to oppose Goring and Grenville, and on the 22nd of that month he came to Windsor to lay down his command and to take leave of the general. But on the following morning he received the commands of the committee to continue his command in spite of the New Ordinance. No direct evidence has yet been produced as to how far Cromwell had arranged his plans for being continued in command, or how far this purpose was generally understood and accepted. It would have been contrary to his nature of restless vigilance and of personal self-reliance, either to commit to chance so momentous an office, or willingly to stand aside out of romantic delicacy. We may doubt the discernment of the worthy Sprigge, when he tells us of the lieutenant-general, "that he thought of nothing less in all the world." Cromwell must have known the counsels of the committee. And doubtless he felt himself so necessary to the cause, and his ascendancy to be so complete, that he might safely leave others to determine the manner and season of his own personal exemption.

The New Model army was now ready; but though Cromwell was continued in command he was not attached to it. For some weeks Cromwell and Fairfax were directed to the west and the Midlands, under orders from London, apparently without aim or general design. We hear of Oliver in Oxfordshire, in Wiltshire, at Ely, and at Huntingdon, in rapid movements of no decisive kind. Fairfax was ordered to meet the king, who, at the end of May, had stormed and sacked Leicester, and was again advancing southwards. Fairfax and his army found the king on the borders of Leicestershire. On the eve of battle, Fairfax sent a letter to the Houses, begging that Cromwell might be sent to command the horse—a service to which he was marked out, wrote the general, by "the general esteem and affection which he hath both with the officers and soldiers of this whole army, his own personal worth and ability for the employment, his great care, diligence, courage, and faithfulness in the services you have already employed him, with the constant presence and blessing of God that have accompanied him." The order demanded was at once sent, and instantly obeyed by Cromwell. In the words of Clarendon: "The evil genius of the kingdom in a moment shifted the whole scene."

The two armies were now in touch; and at six in the morning, 13th June, at Guilsborough, Fairfax held a council of war. "In the midst of the debate," says Sprigge, "came in Lieutenant-General Cromwell, out of the Association, with six hundred horse and dragoons, who was with the greatest joy received by the general and the whole army. Instantly orders were given for drums to beat, trumpets to sound to horse, and all our army to draw to a rendezvous." The arrival of Oliver changed the whole scene. For some days, through both armies, the rumour had run "that 'Ironsides' was coming to join the Parliament's army"; and as he rode in with his eastern troopers the cavalry raised a great shout of joy. Harrison was sent out with one party to scout; Ireton, with another strong force, to watch the enemy's flank. On both sides they made ready for a decisive battle.

On 14th June, at three in the. morning, Fairfax advanced towards Naseby; and at five the king's army was seen cresting the northern hills. Fairfax, with skilful manoeuvres, drew up his army thus. As usual, he placed his foot in the centre. The entire cavalry, near 6000 strong, he committed to Cromwell, who placed them on the two wings—Ireton on the left, with five regiments and dragoons; whilst he himself, with six regiments, took the right wing. As at Marston, the armies were nearly equal, about 10,000 each; the positions not unequal; the general disposition of the armies almost the same. But the tactics and the qualities of the troops are evidently much improved. It is said that the king had 1500 officers who had seen regular war; and Cromwell directed the counsels of Fairfax. As at Marston, Bupert commanded the right wing for the king; but he was no longer opposed to Cromwell, who now led the right wing of the Parliament. The combat in its general features curiously resembled that of Marston, the difference being that at Naseby it is a well-ordered battle between regular troops, and no longer a confused *melee* of militiamen. As at Marston, the centre and one wing of the Parliament were in sore straits, when the wing which Cromwell led, having annihilated the enemy opposed to it, sweeping round, overwhelmed the victorious centre and wing of the royal army, and again snatched victory out of defeat.

As the cavalry of the king were seen to advance with gallantry and resolution, Cromwell, not waiting the attack, charged with his whole wing. The word that day was "*God our strength*." As regiment after regiment charged, they routed and drove back in confusion the king's left wing: "Not one body of the enemy's horse which they charged but they routed." In the meantime the foot in Fairfax's centre were "overpressed," gave ground, and went off in some disorder, falling back on their reserves; when they rallied, and again pressed back on the king.

The left wing of the Parliament, where Ireton was in command, had fared worse. The furious charge of Rupert had broken them in pieces. Ireton, wounded in the thigh and face, was for the time taken prisoner. Rupert pursued the broken wing almost to Naseby, and was making an attempt on the train in the rear, when at last he perceived the disaster that had befallen his left wing on the other side of the field. Cromwell, having driven the enemy's horse in front of him quite behind the infantry, turned round, as at Marston, on the king's centre, which, taken in flank and in front, was speedily dispersed. One *tertia* alone (like Newcastle's border Whitecoats at Marston) held out for the king, "standing with incredible courage and resolution, assailed in flanks, front, and rear," till Cromwell brought up Fairfax's own regiment of foot, who, falling on the remnant with butt-end of muskets as the cavalry plunged into flank and rear, finally broke and destroyed them.

The king still had a strong force of horse, mainly consisting of Rupert's men returning from the chase; and for a moment it seemed that the day had yet to be decided by a fresh combat between the victorious horse on either side. But Cromwell's unshaken wariness, even in the heat of victory, refused to trust so momentous an issue to chance. With signal energy he and Fairfax again brought up the infantry and cannon, and rapidly re-formed the army in a new line, with horse, foot, and guns in regular order of battle. Charles, who now had none but his rallied horsemen to lead, rode round, calling out, "One charge more, gentlemen, and the day is ours." It was too late. His troopers, no longer with infantry or guns, found before them again a solid army advancing in complete order. At the sight "they broke without standing one stroke more." For fourteen miles, up to two miles of Leicester, they were chased; severe execution was done, and crowds of prisoners taken.

It was a crushing defeat. Five thousand prisoners, five hundred of them officers, cannon, train, powder, standards, baggage, and the king's cabinet with his papers, fell to the victors. Politically, the seizure of the papers disclosing the royal intrigues were the most important result of the battle. In a military sense, the king was annihilated. No one numbered the slain. But the king's army had ceased to exist. Rallying a few horsemen he escaped to Leicester, and retreated into the west, never again appearing at the head of an army in the field.

The generals of the Parliament had all fought bravely and commanded with skill. Skippon, the Major-General, and Ireton were severely wounded. Fairfax, without a helmet, led his men in person in the thick of the fight. Cromwell had his morion cut from his head in single combat. On both sides the battle was fought with skill and courage. The preliminary manoeuvres of the Parliament's army were those of scientific war; the rally of the centre and the skilful co-operation of right wing with centre had displayed the discipline and mobility of an organised army. And the rapidity and steadiness with which the second order of battle was improvised bears the infallible stamp of the genius of Cromwell in the field—passionate energy in act, with imperturbable self-command, wariness, and presence of mind.

That very night Cromwell sent off his famous despatch to the Houses, wherein it is easy to see that he treated himself as practically general-in-chief; and in his almost menacing words on behalf of his Independents he is speaking already in the tone of a dictator. To this point he was now visibly arriving. First he creates a troop, then a regiment; soon he creates the Eastern Association and its army; he then develops the Association army into the New Model. The New Model had now concluded the first Civil War. And it was the master of the Parliament; indeed it was itself the real Parliament of the nation. His despatch, sent direct to Speaker, ends thus:

> "Sir—This is none other but the hand of God, and to Him alone belongs the glory, wherein none are to share with Him. The General served you with all faithfulness and honour; and the best commendation I can give him is, That I daresay he attributes all to God, and would rather perish than assume to himself. Which is an honest and a thriving way; and yet as much for bravery may be given to him, in this action, as to a man. Honest men served you faithfully in this action. Sir, they are trusty; I beseech you, in the name of God, not to discourage them. I wish this action may beget thankfulness and humility in all that are concerned in it. He that ventures his life for the liberty of his country, I wish he trust God for the liberty of his conscience, and yon for the liberty he fights for. In this he rests, who is your most humble servant, OLIVER CROMWELL."

For twelve months the army was in the south and west, stamping out what remained to the king in arms; and Cromwell was engaged, for the most part as second to Fairfax, in a constant succession of sieges. In the siege he is the same as in the field—careless of elaborate tactics, preferring direct storm, but ever watchful to adjust ends to means; risking nothing, but always choosing the straightest means which each case presents from hour to hour. In the conduct of a siege his method is historic, and the memory of it long clung round his name. There are few parts of England where one fails to meet some ruined castle or dismantled manor-house, of which the local rumour records "that it was battered down by Cromwell in the troubles." This is his plan. Suddenly appearing in full force before a place, he summons it peremptorily, with the threat to put the defenders to the sword. If this first display of force does not succeed, he chooses a vulnerable point, steadily pours in shot from his cannon till a practicable breach is effected. Then if surrender is offered, he grants it on favourable terms. If not, carefully disposing his force for simultaneous attack, and preparing reserves for the main rush, he makes the signal early for a sudden storm. The storming parties pour in, following each other with desperate energy at all costs till the place is won. Of these sieges the most important was the capture of Bristol and the extinction of Rupert; the most brilliant the storm of Basing, with its carnage and destruction. In the course of some sixteen months (April 1645-August 1646) the historian of the New Model enumerates upwards of sixty successful encounters, about fifty strong places taken, more than 1000 cannon, 40,000 arms, and 250 colours.

During these operations the army was much annoyed by the peasantry. Cromwell's dealing with the Clubmen—bands of half-armed countrymen, numbering some thousands, and playing much the part of the *francs-tireurs* of modern war—was a model of moderation, firmness, and tact. By a mixture of sound argument, vigorous handling, and kindly good sense, he speedily dispersed these troublesome bands—sent "the poor silly creatures" to their homes. Bristol was stormed and taken on the 10th and 11th of September, and the long and exact despatch of Cromwell was by the general's order sent direct to the Speaker Lenthall. It was a large city, regularly entrenched and fortified, held by some 4000 men. The works were far too extensive to be properly invested by so moderate a force. The storm began at one in the morning of the 10th; it was a desperate service, stubbornly contested foot by foot. On the following day Rupert surrendered, and is heard of in arms no more. There were taken 150 cannon, 100 barrels of powder, shot, and arms, and 4000 men. The loss of the Parliament's army was less than 200.

Cromwell's despatch to the Speaker gives us an exact account of these skilful and vigorous operations. And then he abruptly bursts into the famous appeal, so little like the language of a lieutenant-general to a Parliament, or of a soldier to his Government—a veritable sermon, almost an allocation, such as Knox or Latimer might have uttered from the pulpit to their sovereign, almost as a Gregory or an Innocent might have spoken to a feudal prince:

> "Thus I have given you a true, but not a full account of this great business; wherein he that runs may read, That all this is none other than the work of God. He must be a very Atheist who doth not acknowledge it.
>
> "It may be thought that some praises are due to those gallant men, of whose valour so much mention is made:—their humble suit to you and all that have an interest in this blessing, is, That in the remembrance of God's praises they be forgotten. It's their joy that they are instruments of God's glory and their country's good. It's their honour that God vouchsafes to use them. Sir, they that have been employed in this service know, that faith and prayer obtained this City for you: I do not say ours only, but of the people of God with you and all England over, who have wrestled with God for a blessing in this very thing. Our desires are, that God may be glorified by the same spirit of faith by which we ask all our sufficiency, and have received it. It is meet that He have all the praise. Presbyterians, Independents, all have here the same spirit of faith and prayer; the same presence and answer; they agree here, have no names of difference: pity it is it should be otherwise anywhere! All that believe, have the real unity, which is most

> glorious; because inward, and spiritual, in the Body, and to the Head. For being united in forms, commonly called Uniformity, every Christian will for peace-sake study and do, as far as conscience will permit. And for brethren, in things of the mind we look for no compulsion, but that of light and reason. In other things, God hath put the sword in the Parliament's hands,—for the terror of evil-doers, and the praise of them that do well. If any plead exemption from that,—he knows not the Gospel: if any would wring that out of your hands, or steal it from you under what pretence soever, I hope they shall do it without effect. That God may maintain it in your hands, and direct you in the use thereof, is the prayer of your humble servant, OLIVER CROMWELL."

Winchester surrendered on the 6th of October, after two days' bombarding, with 680 men, 7 cannon, with a loss of less than 12 men. "Sir," wrote Cromwell to Fairfax, "this is the addition of another mercy. You see God is not weary in doing you good." The prisoners complained of being robbed contrary to articles. Cromwell had the six men accused tried: all were found guilty, one by lot was hanged, and five were sent to the Royalist governor at Oxford, who returned them "with an acknowledgment of the Lieutenant-General's nobleness."

Basing House, an immense fortress, with a feudal castle and a Tudor palace within its ramparts, had long been a thorn in the side of the Parliament. Four years it had held out, with an army within, well provisioned for years, and blocked the road to the west. At last it was resolved to take it; and Cromwell was directly commissioned by Parliament to the work. Its capture is one of the most terrible and stirring incidents of the war. After six days' constant cannonade, the storm began at six o'clock in the morning of the 14th of October. After some hours of desperate fighting, one after another its defences were taken, and its garrison put to the sword or taken. The plunder was prodigious;

the destruction of property unsparing. It was gutted, burnt, and the very ruins carted away. The night before the storm Cromwell spent much time in prayer,—his chaplain records that "he seldom fights without some text of Scripture to support him." This time his text was from the 115th Psalm—"Not unto us, O Lord, not unto us, but unto thy name give glory, for thy mercy, and for thy truth's sake. . . . Their idols are silver and gold, the work of men's hands. . . . They that make them are like unto them; so is every one that trusteth in them." Basing House was an old "nest of idolatry"; its owner, the Marquis of Winchester, was one of the great chiefs of the Catholics in England. And as Cromwell and his Ironsides stormed into the proud old stronghold and tore it to fragments, they were full of the spirit in which Samuel had hewed Agag in pieces.

Cromwell's despatch to the Speaker is a typical example of many such a piece. "Sir, I thank God," he writes, "I can give you a good account of Basing,"— bursting in on the Parliament with the fury of battle still hot within him. Then comes the clear, quiet, nervous and brief story of the storm. Then a paragraph full of strategic sagacity, urging and almost dictating the immediate razing of the fortress. "Sir, I hope not to delay, but to march towards the west to-morrow." Then the repeated appeals to the House in the tone of a preacher not a soldier, which in Cromwell's mouth most certainly were not idle phrases—

> "The Lord grant that these mercies may be acknowledged with all. thankfulness: God exceedingly abounds in His goodness to us, and will not be weary until righteousness and peace meet, and until He hath brought forth a glorious work for the happiness of this poor kingdom, wherein desires to serve God and you with a faithful heart your most humble servant, OLIVER CROMWELL."

Castle after castle, town after town, regiment after regiment surrendered, as Cromwell and Fairfax rode fast and struck hard from side to side. In March, Sir Ralph Hopton, with 4000 men, 2000 arms, and 20 colours, surrendered in Cornwall; and Sir Jacob Astley, the last commander in the field, in Gloucestershire. In April Donnington Castle was taken: and now the king, wandering aimlessly about, surrendered himself to the Scots at Newark. Oxford, with some 3000 men and 300 cannon, surrendered in June, and Ragland Castle in August 1646.

The First Civil War was over.

CHAPTER VI

BETWEEN THE CIVIL WARS

A.B. 1646–1648. AETAT. 47–49

The three years which elapsed between the defeat of the king and his death on the scaffold (1646-49) are the most intricate and obscure of the Civil War, and they form the period in which the action of Cromwell can be least definitely traced. It was a long triangular duel between the king, the Parliament, and the army: the king, with wonderful pertinacity and no little subtlety, intriguing to recover his authority intact; the Houses bent on formal Parliamentary government and Presbyterian despotism; the army bent on real constitutional guarantees and liberty of conscience. The main struggle lay between the Parliament and the army: the main question being Presbyterian orthodoxy, or Bible freedom. But the dead weight of conservatism that still clung round the fallen monarchy, and the unflagging ingenuity of Charles, made the Crown still a powerful factor in the contest; whilst the political interests were far too real to be long merged in any religious quarrel. Parliament was controlled by Presbyterians, who, in their eagerness to secure Presbyterian ascendancy, were ready to restore the monarchy with merely nominal guarantees. The army, which consisted mainly of Independents, and was inspired by men who were zealots for civil and religious freedom, was resolved to prevent—if need be by force— either

Presbyterian domination or restoration of the old monarchy. As Charles wrote to Digby with no little astuteness, he hoped to draw either the Presbyterians or the Independents "to side with me for extirpating one another, and I shall be really king again." In the end, after three years of intricate manoeuvres conducted on all sides with great audacity and craft, the army won, forced the Parliament to become their tool, and brought the king to the block.

A course of policy so complex and shifting cannot be set forth in the limits of this *Life*. And as the part which was played in it by Cromwell is still traceable only by indirect evidence, and was constantly varied by the progress of events, it cannot be stated otherwise than in general outline. The plan of this book does not admit of the discussion of authorities or the narrative of events in which Cromwell himself intervened occasionally and indirectly. It was beyond his power to do more than this. As pre-eminently a practical statesman, and what is now called an opportunist, he had no settled policy, no doctrine, no single purpose to achieve. He struck in, first here, then there, as occasion arose; changing his tactics and his objects as new combinations or fresh situations developed. Although an Independent to the backbone, and siding essentially with the army, he is far too large a statesman not to see the strong points both of king and of Parliament—not to feel all the evils of a revolutionary army. He stands above all parties, alternately using all and controlling all.

Nor is there any problem more difficult than exactly to follow Cromwell's policy in all its details. For this part of his life there is exceedingly little direct and unimpeachable authority. There is a large body of disconnected anecdotes, more or less resting on contemporary authorities, mostly hostile, of very various trustworthiness, and all capable of different explanations. They are for the most part so characteristic and plausible that it is difficult to doubt but that they rest at bottom on fact. But the time, place, circumstances of them are all-important, as are the facts that led up to them, and which followed them; and it is just in these that the authority of the "Memoirs" is least satisfactory. The result of a patient balancing of authorities is all that can here be given. Much must be left to the estimate we form of Cromwell as a whole. The probabilities are all on the side of a belief that the ultimate result was mainly shaped by him; that all the critical turns in this long and arduous political game were inspired by his genius, and bear marks of his mastery over men.

This too is the point at which we first note complaints of his ambition, duplicity, and intrigue; his abandonment by his early friends; and the public and private animosities which continued to gather round him, growing throughout the rest of his life. It is the too familiar story of the great man in a troubled crisis. And no statesman of equal rank in the modern history of Europe comes forth from the ordeal of disparagement more nobly. Through all these tangled times Oliver Cromwell remains unswervingly true to his great design: to secure responsible government without anarchy, and freedom of conscience without intolerance. These great ends were to him far dearer than parties, institutions, or persons; and for them he would sacrifice in turn parties, institutions, and persons. If he could have saved responsible government without destroying the monarchy, he would have done it. If he could have established a Parliamentary system without misrule and religious oppression, he would have done it. Had he desired an army despotism, he would have worked it out directly, without reference to Parliament or king. Had he aimed at personal power, he would not have risked life and popularity so often in the cause of law, order, and Parliament.

But it is not given to human genius to guide a seething revolution to a great issue without wounding to the heart even good and honest men; without resorting to methods which are not those of perfect saintliness; without reticence, suspicion, change of purpose, much secret counsel, and much using of men to the point where they cease to be useful. Irritation, opposition, calumny are the natural result. And the greater the superiority of the leader to his contemporaries, the more profound is the opposition and misunderstanding he meets. For all his mighty brain and great soul, Oliver Cromwell was no perfect hero, or spotless saint. Doubtless the fine edge of candour was rudely worn down by a long career of indirect policy. The master of men is never wholly amiable or absolutely frank. The man who often changes his front in the heat of battle always seems a time-server to duller minds. The man who takes up the task for which he knows himself only to be fit, always seems ambitious to those whom he thrusts aside.

Nor was Cromwell without the defects of his qualities. A somewhat coarse humour arid a weakness for horseplay sat strangely on a man who was certainly consumed within with profound and silent designs. The habit of extempore expounding cannot be indulged without harm. And doubtless the taste for improving the occasion became at last a snare to Cromwell, ending even with him, as it ended with others, in no little unction, mannerism—even self-deception. A certain profusion of tears, of hyperbolic asseverations and calling God to witness, an excessive expression of each passing emotion which grew with the habit of spiritual stimulants—these are things too well attested and too consonant with the tone of his generation to suffer us to doubt that Cromwell's nature was more than touched by the disease. It was touched, but not poisoned. He had some of the weakness as well as all the strength of the mighty Puritanism of which he is the incarnation and the hero. But all these unlovely failings, which in truthfulness we note, disappear in a larger view of the essential grandeur, sincerity, and devoutness of the man.

The relative strength of the three parties was this. By his defeat and imprisonment, Charles gained rather then lost the moral strength of his position. Men no longer feared his vengeance as a conqueror; they were no longer irritated by the outrages of his soldiers; he had lost his dangerous power, but he was still lawful king. The great majority of the nation could imagine no stable government except in the king's name; the legal and executive machinery was hardly workable without him. Captivity put an end to his arbitrary acts, and gave scope for his personal dignity and courage. He still retained the passionate devotion of Church, aristocracy, and large sections of the countrypeople. Nay, we are accustomed to rate the ability of Charles Stuart too low. Cromwell said: "The king is a man of great parts and great understanding." In truth Charles showed, both in peace and war, singular tenacity, a very shrewd eye for a difficult situation, and a curious subtlety in intrigue, akin to that of an Italian statesman. Had he been Pope or Spanish governor, dealing with Italians or Flemings, it is quite likely that he would have won. His incurable weakness was that he never shook off the Machiavellian or Medicean "Prince," and never understood the nature of Englishmen.

The House of Commons was now in its seventh year, and had lost touch with the country. Reduced by withdrawals and expulsions to a mere shadow of itself, it had partly filled up its ranks by new elections which were neither legal nor regular. Its constitutional position, which in the midst of war had been accepted of necessity, was incurably bad as a normal institution. An assembly which recognised the right of none to dissolve it, which had ejected a majority of its own members, and which had governed for years by arbitrary decrees enforced, if at all, by the power of the sword, was little more than a revolutionary committee. Both Houses, or what remained of them, were controlled by fanatical Presbyterians, by officers discarded at the New Model, by self-important lawyers, and city magnates. But Parliament still possessed three great advantages. The victories had been won by its soldiers in its name; it had the sole command of the taxing power; and it was the one constitutional authority remaining. It had still in its ranks bold, able, and sincere men; it had the devoted support of London and the Presbyterian clergy. Its weakness was this—that whilst its claim to sovereignty could only be admitted in a state of war, it no longer represented the country, and was openly hostile to the power which had defeated Charles.

That power was the army, the flower of all that was earnest, brave, and zealous in Puritanism: men who for years had fought, bled, and submitted to the sternest discipline for the Cause, at their own cost, and without hope of reward. They were what in continental theories would be known as the "active citizens" in the great contest; wont to discuss, pray, and preach over every occasion. Such an army of volunteers, carefully selected by their officers on Cromwell's own model, all uncongenial elements being gradually weeded out, men who in scores of combats had never known one defeat, as soldiers had endured an iron discipline for years, but as citizens and Christians had been encouraged to debate every incident of the day. They thus united the combative enthusiasm of the Protestant martyrs to the skill and experience of Caesar's legionaries. Though as troopers the world has never seen their superiors, they remained politicians and zealots of intense activity. As the war closed and the struggle between them and the Parliament grew acute, they formed themselves into an organised political body. The officers formed a council; and the men chose delegates, two for each company or troop, known as Agitators.

This organisation could hardly have existed without Cromwell's approval. And there is every reason to believe that he promoted, if he did not originate it. He recognised, supported, and worked with it: mainly using Ireton as his agent. Every step in the negotiations was referred to this double council, which regularly consulted its constituents in the ranks. It was thus a real Parliament; much more truly representative than that at Westminster, better organised, and with more political alertness. It was indeed more truly in touch with the voting power in the kingdom. The subsidiary elections to Parliament had returned an immense majority of men in sympathy with the Independents, and amongst them Fairfax, Ludlow, Ireton, Fleetwood, Blake, Sidney, and Hutchinson. A force like this, more than twenty thousand strong, with such leaders and with all the prestige of victory and unbroken success, were the true masters of England. Even as a representative and political body, they were morally stronger than the remnant at Westminster. What they lacked was any legal or constitutional right. Of this they were quite conscious. They were ready to recognise to the full, and even to overrate, the legal and constitutional right of the Parliament. The name of "the Commons of England" still overawed them.

But the struggle between the Parliament and the army was not a mere contest of Law against the Sword, Right against Might. Both Parliament and army were revolutionary bodies, formed out of the exigencies of civil war. The army had no legal right, and they claimed none. But they had a preponderance of moral right to represent the victorious side, almost as great as their preponderance of material force. From the point of view of law, the Parliament which now sat in Westminster had scarcely more technical right than the army; yet they exercised arbitrary powers which the cessation of war made every day more irregular. But the Revolution, which had arisen out of legal problems, and had so long been carried on under the forms of ancient law and custom, was still for three years longer continued under the semblance of quasi-constitutional methods. And no men felt this more thoroughly than Cromwell and the chiefs of the army. The Parliament, therefore, still remained, at least in name, the official embodiment of the nation.

Cromwell returned to Parliament on the 23rd of April 1646, whilst the king was still at the head of an army in Oxford, and still had forces and castles in various places. The Lieutenant-General was received with honours and rewards. From thenceforth for more than a year his activity is mainly in Parliament, from whence he watches and influences events. In the army he was the second man in rank and the first in repute. In the House of Commons he was hardly in the first line and was surrounded by bitter enemies. It is inconceivable that a general, bent on founding a military dictatorship, would have left the army, in the act of reaping the fruits of its victories, to place himself in a Parliament where he never publicly shone. But Parliament was the proper authority to conclude the struggle; and Parliament, rightly advised, had the power to do so. No sooner was the king in the hands of the Scots than all men perceived the importance of controlling his person, and getting rid of the Scotch army. The disbanding of the army, the establishment of Presbyterianism, the control of the king, and the return home of the Scots— all rested alike with Parliament. To the House, therefore, came Cromwell, but more to confer than to speak.

It was at this epoch in his career that Cromwell married two of his daughters, and arranged for the marriage of his eldest son, in families of his own rank: simple country gentlemen, devoted to the cause. Bridget married Ireton, Cromwell's "other self"; Elizabeth married John Claypole—both in 1646. Richard's marriage to Dorothy Mayor was proposed in 1647, but not carried out till 1649, on the eve of the Irish campaign. They were not the alliances that a Bonaparte would have sought. In 1646 the Cromwell household removed from Ely to London, and were modestly lodged in Westminster.

During the long and intricate negotiations between the king, the Parliament, and the Scots, the army and the Independents looked on with anxiety and watchfulness, but did not actively interfere. That was also the attitude of Cromwell, who formed the connecting link between Parliament and the army. From brief sentences in his letters, and from the less trustworthy source of the "Memoirs," we gather that the Lieutenant-General watched with indignation the growing hostility to the army amongst the Parliamentary leaders, the Presbyterians, and the city. Had the king accepted the Covenant and the terms of Parliament, the cause of the Independents, and, indeed, the future of England, might have been at stake. One who knew Charles would have rested easy that this was impossible; and though a doubtful story suggests that Cromwell had secretly encouraged the king to refuse the terms of the Parliament, it was sufficiently notorious that the Independents would not have required him to accept the Covenant. Cromwell appears to have concurred in the efforts to pay and get rid of the Scots. And this was successfully accomplished in January 1647.

So soon as the Scots were paid off and had returned home, leaving the king with the Parliament, a direct conflict ensued between the Houses and the army. To disband the army was to crush Independency (which then was practically Dissent) and to neutralise the Generals (who had so great extra-Parliamentary authority). And thus the disbanding of the army was the dominant idea of the Presbyterian leaders in Parliament. In March they began to raise a new force to defend the city against the army. "There want not, in all places," wrote Cromwell to Fairfax, "men who have so much malice against the army as besots them." And in the same month the advisers of the army were declared by Parliament to be "enemies of the State." From this hour the army was in a mutinous attitude, refusing: to disband till its demands were satisfied, and so it continued for six months till Parliament submitted.

Cromwell's task was indeed a difficult one. No soldier had ever a greater horror of mutiny, and no statesman more completely understood that the settlement of the kingdom must be at once legal and Parliamentary. The army had force; but it could put no pressure on the king, and could not grant to itself indemnities and arrears. The work of Cromwell was so to use the army as to compel the Parliament to come to a settlement in a certain way, and yet not to set up the anarchy of an armed mob. Backwards and forwards he passes during April and May between army and Parliament, moderating and guiding the demands of the army, and presenting them to Parliament in their least offensive light. It became manifest that the Presbyterian leaders in their hostility to the army were prepared to make any terms with the king; there was even talk of arresting Cromwell. Charles and the Parliament together, if they had come to terms, could have made a legal settlement, which for the moment would have been accepted by the nation, leaving every question open and every soldier who had fought in the war liable for treason. A series of rapid and bold strokes changed the whole aspect of affairs.

On the 2nd of June Cromwell suddenly left London for the army, and on that same day a strong body of horse under Joyce, a cornet of Fairfax's guard, took the king out of the custody of the Parliament's commissioners, and with every show of respect carried him off to the army. On the 4th took place a brilliant review; and within a few days the whole army, 21,000 strong, was gathered round Newmarket. Thence, on the 10th, they issued their famous Manifesto, and marching, to St. Albans, openly threatened the city and Parliament. The Manifesto, held to be Cromwell's own draft, demanded satisfaction for themselves, the removal of their accusers, and a real settlement of the kingdom before they were themselves disbanded. The army threatened, and waited at a respectful distance; but the threat was not enough. The city became a prey to confusion; the House of Commons was invaded by a city mob; yet neither Parliament nor city gave way. Thereupon the army marched on in earnest. On 3rd of August it occupied and entered London. The Speaker and the Independent leaders sought refuge with the army; the Presbyterian leaders withdrew; the city was respectful; and the House of Commons yielded.

Thus, on the 3rd of August 1647, the army visibly assumed the chief authority in the State. Fairfax was solemnly received and thanked by Parliament; the troops marched, crowned with laurel branches, through the streets to Westminster, and then through the city, every approach being occupied in military fashion. As the victors of Marston, Naseby, and Basing tramped through London in splendid array and perfect discipline, horse, foot, and artillery, with drums, trumpets, and colours, "in so civil and orderly a manner, that not the least offence or prejudice was offered by them to any man, either in words, action, or gestures, as they marched," the citizens were at once reassured and overawed. They saw before them an organised body of men, irresistible in strength, and resolved to carry out their purpose, but with no element of' disorder or personal motive. From this day, in fact, the Parliament had visibly ceased to be sovereign. It accepted a master, and consented to lend its name to the decision of others.

This was the real "usurpation" and military dictatorship. But it was accomplished officially by Fairfax in person. The names of Parliament and of Constitution too often dispose men to treat this act as an invasion of legal authority by the sword. It was undoubtedly an act of force and of revolution. But so was the entire Civil War. Neither Parliament nor army had strict law on their side, nor a clear majority of the nation. But the cause that the army represented was the higher and the truer: the cause which has ultimately prevailed.

Both Parliament and army appealed to force, and the force of the army was immeasurably the greater. The part which Cromwell took in this series of events is not yet quite proved; but there is every reason to believe that it was all in the main essentially his work. No general order could issue to the army without the knowledge and assent of Fairfax, Cromwell, and Ireton. These three were practically one.

Cromwell was now called in the pamphlets *Dominus factotum*. The mysterious seizure of the king, with the simultaneous muster at Newmarket, the army Manifesto, and the march on London, were all master-strokes—timed, concerted, and executed with the unity and precision of a great strategist. The abduction of the king showed a genius for manoeuvre, and the triumphal march through the city showed a mastery of explosive forces, such as mark but one man only in that age. And those who incline to see merely the intriguing ambition of a tyrant must remember that it was the policy approved by Fairfax, Ireton, Fleetwood, Hutchinson, Milton, and thousands of the most single-minded heroes who ever entered into civic strife.

The surrender of the Parliament and possession of the king entirely changed the position of the army, and with it the policy of Cromwell. The army chiefs had encouraged political action amongst the soldiers, but they were now anxious to moderate it; whilst they laboured to reconcile the Presbyterian and Independent parties, and to come to terms directly with the king. So momentous a work as the making such an army the visible master of England could not be carried through without grave political and social consequences. A strong and earnest party of Commonwealth's men contained some of the most honourable of the Puritans, such as Vane, Ludlow, Sidney, Hutchinson, Milton, and Marvell. But in the army was found the hotbed and centre not only of the Commonwealth, but of various political and social movements, showing neatly all the phases of new ideas which the history of later revolutions has made familiar. The most definite of these groups were the party known as Levellers, who, in spite of their nickname, did not maintain Communism, but what in modern political language is known as the doctrine of Political Equality.

The army had long played the part of the "clubs" and "sections" in the French revolutions; of the "leagues" and "associations" of English reform; and nearly every type of modern radicalism was duly represented in the army demands, short, perhaps, of formal Socialism. Republicanism, sovereignty of Parliament, annual or biennial elections, extension and equalisation of the suffrage, local self-government, codification of the law, complete religious liberty, and equal political rights, were repeatedly pressed on Parliament and proclaimed as rights. And now the army was becoming the real House of Commons. The Parliament occupied relatively the position we are wont to attribute to the present House of Lords—an assembly without which a legal settlement is impossible, but which, in the long run, must virtually submit to the more popular authority. Now Cromwell was a statesman, not a theorist. Though an enemy of arbitrary monarchy, and ever eager for practical reform, he had no leaning in principle either to a republic or a democracy. He was by temper and conviction no radical. Circumstances, indeed, made him what, by a happy paradox, has been called "a conservative revolutionist." Thus it came to pass that no sooner was the army master, than Cromwell laboured to control it.

Turning a deaf ear to Levellers and Commonwealth's men, Cromwell was engaged for months in the effort to make terms with the king directly. Communications had probably begun even before the seizure of the king by Joyce, an act to which Charles showed little objection and hardly even surprise. But when the victorious army carried the king about with them, Cromwell and Ireton were in daily relations with him. The task they undertook was transcendently difficult, if not impossible. They had to find a basis of settlement which the king would accept, and yet one that the army would not reject; and then, if king and army agreed, it would have to be adopted by the Parliament, which alone could make a legal settlement. For months the subtle and inventive brains of the two generals were pitted against the incurable perfidy of the Stuart; and the personal relations between the fallen sovereign and his rebel officers became not only courteous, but intimate and friendly. The troopers saw with increasing irritation their great general becoming a courtier, and almost a confidential adviser of the king. If the anecdote-mongers may be trusted, Cromwell loudly expressed his warm interest in the king, not only as a man, but as an institution. He is reported to have said that no men could enjoy their lives and estates quietly without the king had his rights. The grumblings of the army swelled into open accusations, and even, it is said, into plots to assassinate Charles and Cromwell. Things reached such a pitch that he was forced to stop the public access to himself of the king's agents. But still he struggled on to replace Charles on his throne by a legal settlement of the nation.

Why did he make an effort so obstinate and so dangerous? Why did he abandon it, and as eagerly work for the king's dethronement and execution? The exact steps in his policy are not quite traced, but the general course of it is plain. Cromwell was a man who by temper and opinion was perfectly willing to accept the monarchic and social constitution as he found it, up to the point where it became impracticable or mischievous. He was not given to visions of a future, and not eager after new constitutions. He still believed that the republicans were a small minority, and that English society was not workable without a monarchy. Cromwell, like so many great statesmen, was never in the van of the movement, but always just ahead of the central force. He was now, in 1647, convinced that there could be no settlement without a king. And he risked reputation, power, and life, to effect a settlement with the king.

Having strained his influence almost to the bursting point, he suddenly changed front. Nearly all through 1647 we find him negotiating a monarchic settlement. Early in 1648 he denounced the king in Parliament. What explains the change? Two things essentially. The growing violence of the Commonwealth party in the army; and the conviction that the king was intriguing, not for a settlement at all, but for a new civil war. Long and ominous were the warnings that told Cromwell the temper of the army. His own life, that of Charles, a new war, a military revolt, the solution of all discipline were at stake. The mutiny at Ware could not but cost the general much cruel searching of heart. His severity was "absolutely necessary," as he told Ludlow, "to keep things from falling into confusion." On 15th November two regiments appeared at a review without orders and with mutinous papers in their hats, with the motto "England's freedom and soldiers' rights." Cromwell, with a few officers, rode up to them, and with thunder in his brow, ordered them to take out the papers. One regiment obeyed; the other refused. Ordering eleven men from the ranks by name, he tried them on the spot by court-martial, condemned three to death, and shot one. It was a terrible moment; which must have burnt its lessons into the army and into the general.

On the other hand, Cromwell at last fathomed the perfidy of the king. Charles held himself to be one who was by divine ordinance incapable of binding himself by any agreement. The famous story of the letter to the queen concealed in a saddle which Cromwell and Ireton discovered, though it professes to come from Cromwell's own lips, may or may not be true in its details; but it is the picturesque expression of an important truth. Cromwell, with or without intercepted letters, at last discovered that the king was only playing with him in all these negotiations for a settlement, whilst he was really occupied in stirring up a new war. Once satisfied of this, Cromwell turned upon Charles Stuart the whole force of his loathing and enmity. Cromwell was accustomed, both earlier and later, to deal with astute men, and to meet them on equal terms in tortuous and secret paths. He was himself far from being an Israelite without guile. He had probably by this time persuaded himself that in diplomacy, as in war, stratagems with an opponent are lawful parts of the game. He, no doubt, did not show Charles his whole mind; nor did he expect Charles to show his whole mind to him. But with the king it was different. The king in these long negotiations was not negotiating at all; he was only laying a trap. He was solemnly debating a treaty, when he never intended to keep any treaty at all. And this at last Cromwell came to see was not diplomacy, but incurable perfidy.

Nor was it merely the perfidy of a helpless prisoner. The Scotch Presbyterians were now brought round to the side of their king. A large body in Parliament were once more inclined to the same result. In east, west, and north cavaliers were again arming. And between a Scotch invasion, new Royalist musters, intrigues in Parliament, and Presbyterian jealousy, the army was in imminent peril that they and their cause would perish. The near prospect of the Second Civil War decided all. And now, with all that he had fought for at stake, with a fresh tide of blood rising, with the army itself in chronic mutiny, and the noblest spirits in the army clamouring incessantly for "justice," Cromwell at last gave way; resolved to strike down the throne, the rallying point of all disorder; and to bring to trial the "man of blood," who, in spite of every effort, was obstinately bent on renewing the war.

Dark and fierce were the prayers and outpourings of heart with which the Ironsides sought the Lord as the Second Civil War gathered round them. The fiery words of the Hebrew prophets had heated their brains; and the Biblical notions of "atonement" and "the avenger of blood" had grown into sacred moral obligations. To their morbid fanaticism the cause of bloodguiltiness lay upon the land, until he on whose doorpost it rested had atoned for his sins. With the vivid consciousness that each of them might yet be called to answer with his neck before the earthly judge, was mingled a real awe of the heavenly tribunal, if they suffered the guilt to cry aloud in the land. The Second Civil War seemed a judgment on their slackness and the carnal policy of their leaders. And as they buckled on their armour for a fresh campaign they resolved, amidst prayers and maledictions, that if the Lord brought them back in peace, the Chief Delinquent should be called to account.

CHAPTER VII

SECOND CIVIL WAR – TRIAL OF THE KING

A.D. 1648–1649. AETAT. 49

The Second Civil-War broke out in April, and proved to be a short but formidable affair. The whole of Wales was speedily in insurrection; a strong force of cavaliers were mustering in the north of England; in Essex, Surrey, and the southern counties various outbreaks arose; Berwick, Carlisle, Chester, Pembroke, Colchester, were held for the king; the fleet revolted; and 40,000 men were ordered by the Parliament of Scotland to invade England. Lambert was sent to the north; Fairfax to take Colchester; and Cromwell into Wales, and thence to join Lambert and meet the Scotch. On the 24th of May Cromwell reached Pembroke, but being short of guns, he did not take it till 11th July. The rising in Wales crushed, Cromwell turned northwards, where the north-west was already in revolt, and 20,000 Scots, under the Duke of Hamilton, were advancing into the country. Want of supplies and shoes, and sickness, detained him with his army, some 7000 strong, "so extremely harassed with hard service and long marches, that they seemed rather fit for a hospital than a battle." Having joined Lambert in Yorkshire he fought the battle of Preston on 17th of August.

The battle of Preston was one of the most decisive and important victories ever gained by Cromwell, over the most numerous enemy he ever encountered, and the first in which he was in supreme command. Although the enemy's forces were nearly threefold his, well-armed, and of high courage, so great was the disparity in military skill, that it was rather a prolonged massacre than a battle. The engagements continued over three days, and nearly thirty miles of country. In the end the entire army of nearly 24,000 good troops were either killed, taken, or dispersed. Early on the morning of the 17th August Cromwell, with some 9000 men, fell upon the army of the Duke of Hamilton unawares, as it proceeded southwards in a long straggling, unprotected line. The invaders consisted of 17,000 Scots and 7000 good men from northern counties. The long ill-ordered line was cut in half and rolled back northward and southward, before they even knew that Cromwell was upon them. The great host, cut into sections, fought with desperation from town to town. But for three days it was one long chase and carnage, which ended only with the exhaustion of the victors and their horses. Ten thousand prisoners were taken. "We have killed we know not what," writes Cromwell, "but a very great number; having done execution upon them above thirty miles together, besides what we killed in the two great fights." His own loss was small, and but one superior officer.

The despatches of the general ring with the heat of battle and chase. It was no longer civil war; it was the extermination of a host of alien invaders, whose success would have been the final ruin of the Cause.

> "It pleased God to enable us to give them a defeat; which I hope we shall improve, by God's assistance, to their utter ruin. . . . The invading army," he writes, "is dissipated. . . . In order to perfecting this work, we desire you to raise your Country; and to improve your forces to the total ruin of that Enemy, which way soever they go; and if you shall accordingly do your part, doubt not of their total ruin. . . . Thus you have their infantry totally ruined. ... We have

> quite tired our horses in pursuit of the enemy: we have killed and disabled all their foot; and left them only some horse. ... If my horse could but trot after them, I would take them all. . . . Let all the counties about you be sent to, to rise with you and follow them."

It was, in very truth, the sword of the Lord and of Gideon. The largest army that ever gathered under the standard of King Charles had been utterly dissipated by a series of blows, swift, crushing, and unsparing.

The Scottish invaders dispersed, Cromwell hastened to recover Berwick and Carlisle, and to restore the Presbyterian or Whig party in Scotland. He advanced to Edinburgh, with abundant professions of his peaceful purpose, and with great precautions to enforce the strictest discipline. He entered Scotland, not as an invader, but as the ally of the party headed by the Marquis of Argyle, in opposition to the Duke of Hamilton. His task there was precisely that of the foreign general who interferes in the factions of the Greek or Italian republics to restore the "good" party and overawe the "bad" party. After a stay of a few weeks he took over Berwick and Carlisle, and advanced into Yorkshire, to recover Pontefract Castle. This he found too strong to be taken without a regular siege train. He remained before Pontefract some weeks. But the train not arriving, he hastened to London, where the great crisis at last was imminent. It is from Yorkshire in this autumn that he writes those striking letters which open to us the very depths of his soul.

To Cromwell the Second Civil War was the unpardonable sin. God had manifested His will in the triumph of the army. To be slack, to be indulgent, was to struggle against His will. To struggle against that manifestation was to tempt God.

> "Sir," he wrote on the battlefield of Preston, "this is nothing but the hand of God." To St. John he writes, "Let us all be not careful what men will make of these actings. They, will they, nill they, shall fulfil the good pleasure of

> God; and we—shall serve our generations. Our rest we expect elsewhere: that will be durable." And then he tells how the poor godly man, dying the day before the battle, taking a handful of cut grass, said, "So too shall wither the army of the Scots," and immediately died. Parliament, he writes to Lord Wharton, does not seem conscious of the crisis. The victory at Preston he calls "this manifest token of His displeasure." "His most righteous witnessing against the army under Duke Hamilton." The bringing in of that army was "a more prodigious Treason than any that had been perfected before: ... it is the repetition of the same offence against all the witnesses that God has borne." His officers, he says, "are amazed to see their blood held so cheap, and such manifest witnessings of God, so terrible and so just, no more reverenced." And to Fairfax he writes: "I find in the officers of the regiments a very great sense of the sufferings of this poor kingdom; and in them all a very great zeal to have impartial justice done upon offenders. And I must confess, I do in all, from my heart concur with them; and I verily think and am persuaded they are things which God puts into our hearts" (20th November 1648).

The Ironsides were returning home to keep their word: and Cromwell was now as deeply resolved as any man to exact the uttermost farthing.

Of all the writings of Cromwell which have been preserved to us, the long letter to Colonel Hammond, of 25th November 1648, best reveals to us his inmost heart, in the very turning-point of his career. If ever a letter was the secret outpouring of the spirit to a beloved friend, it is this. If ever a difficult duty in a momentous crisis awaited a great statesman, it was now.

> "Dear Robin," he writes to his young friend, the king's custodian at Newport, "no man rejoiceth more to see a line from thee than myself." He touches on his recent victories: "We have not been without our share of beholding some remarkable providences, and appearances of the Lord." His young friend was troubled,—had scruples about

the king, about the army dictating to Parliament, about a minority forcing a majority. "Dear Robin," he writes, "thou and I were never worthy to be door-keepers in this Service. If thou wilt seek, seek to know the mind of God in all that chain of Providence." As to Parliament being a lawful authority, "Yes," he says, "but authorities may not do anything, and yet claim obedience. Is not *Salus Populi* a sound position? Is it provided for in the pretended Treaty with the king? Is not the whole fruit of the war like to be frustrated? Is not this army a lawful power, called by God to oppose and fight against the king upon some stated grounds? And may it not oppose one Name of Authority, as well as another name? . . . My dear Friend," he goes on, "let us look into providences; surely they mean somewhat. They hang so together; have been so constant, so clear, unclouded." And then he argues the principle of passive obedience to the Parliament. "Mark how Providence turns the heart of so many against it." He knows "not one officer among them, who is not with them. The difficulties and the enemies against them are not few, are all that is glorious in this world. The recent protest of the army against any treaty with the king may have been premature; but now it is out let us support it. Is the taking action in support of it a tempting of God, as the young Colonel seems to fear? No! Dear Robin, tempting of God is by acting presumptuously or in unbelief. Not the encountering of difficulties, makes us tempt God; but acting without faith. The treaty is 'a ruining hypocritical agreement.' Can we have good from 'this Man—against whom the Lord hath witnessed?'" A great crisis was at hand, and Cromwell earnestly seeks to win his young friend, "because my soul loves thee, and I would not have thee swerve."

The letter did not find Hammond at Newport; and Cromwell having despatched it, hurried to London, where the great drama of king and Parliament was closing to its climax.

On 20th of November the army by Colonel Ewer presented to Parliament its protest against the "hypocritical agreement" with the king. On the 25th it backed this up by advancing to Windsor. On the 27th Colonel Ewer removed Colonel Hammond from his duty about the king, and the following day he removed the king to the mainland and secured him in Hurst Castle. Charles was now for the first time a real prisoner. On the 30th the House rejects the "Remonstrance"; and the army marches upon London, which it reaches on Saturday, 2nd December, and quietly quarters itself round Whitehall. On Monday, 4th, as if in defiance of the army, the House approved the Newport treaty, after an all-night sitting. On Wednesday the 6th, Colonel Rich's regiment of horse were paraded in Palace Yard, Colonel Pride's regiment of foot in Westminster Hall. There Colonel Pride, with Lord Grey as his prompter, arrests forty-one members, and on the following day more than sixty others. This is "Pride's Purge." Cromwell came to town that night, when the first act was over. He declared that "he had not been acquainted with this design; yet since it was done he was glad of it, and would endeavour to maintain it." The next day he received the thanks of the House, whilst the Purge was completed at its doors.

"Pride's Purge" was the most revolutionary of the three great acts of force by which the army coerced the Parliament. In August 1647 Parliament submitted to the will of the army without actual force being used, and without breach of any constitutional form. Cromwell's dismissal of the Rump in April 1652 was the virtual dissolution of the mere ghost of a Parliament by a *de facto* dictator. But Pride's Purge was bare military violence, like any modern *coup d'état*. It was carried out under orders from headquarters, with the consent and in the name of Fairfax, the Commander-in-Chief, by the general's staff, and was mainly contrived by Ireton and Ludlow. Cromwell, like Fairfax, adopted and accepted it; but he did not direct it. He probably was not consulted; or Ludlow, his old enemy, who gives us all the secret consultations, would have told us so. During these rapid transactions he was busy with his army in the north, and had been absent from headquarters for seven months. His letter to Hammond shows that he did not know of the colonel's dismissal, and that he thought the Remonstrance premature. There is no direct evidence of the part which Cromwell took in the army proceedings of the autumn of 1648. Yet he could not have left them with unconcern. What probably happened was this. There was an understanding between the generals in May that the army should have its way, if need be by force. On general matters, Cromwell was consulted and advised. But so far as he was concerned, he probably was content to leave overt action, the time, the mode, and the persons, to Fairfax, his commander, and to Ireton, his "other self."

It is with Pride's Purge in 1648, and not with Cromwell's dismissal in 1653, that the Long Parliament of 1640 virtually ends. Three hundred and fifty members voted in the division which occasioned it. The divisions after it did not exceed fifty-three. The House, its officials, those who sat in it, and those who accepted its decisions, after such an act as that of 6th December, were plainly content to accept the name of Parliament without the reality.

The purging of the House was the means to bring about the will of the army. And the will of the army was to close the era of timorous compromise by bringing to judgment "the man of blood." The trial, condemnation, and beheading of the king belong to the History of England, and not to the Life of Cromwell. It was essentially the act of the army, and in a special sense of Ireton. It was not Cromwell's own conception, nor did he easily adopt it. He long struggled against it, risked life and reputation in the combat. At length he gave way, probably about the time of the second outbreak of war. The Scottish invasion, the victory at Preston, the very catastrophe of the invaders decided him. And in the overwhelming defeat of the Royalists he saw the finger of God pointing to judgment on the contriver of all these horrors. Having taken up this duty, and seeing Parliament prostrate by no direct act of his own, he became one of the keenest and most obdurate of all the judges of the Stuart.

In the Court of Justice Oliver is always present. In the death-warrant of 29th January 1649, next after the President and Lord Grey, stands the name of Oliver Cromwell. He accepted the responsibility of it, justified, defended it to his dying day. No man in England was more entirely answerable for the deed than he. "I tell you," he said to Algernon Sidney, "we will cut off his head with the crown upon it." Traditions tell that he pressed other officers to sign, that he smeared Henry Marten's face with ink as he signed, and stood by the coffin and gazed upon the corpse. It may be, for Cromwell was strange, passionate, and stern in supreme moments; and he knew better than others all that this portentous deed implied.

To him and to his Ironsides to bring the king to judgment was no mere act of earthly justice; it was a sacred duty enjoined by the inward voice and outward signs of God Himself. To show mercy to this Agag was flagrant rebellion against God's will. For seven years the land had swam in blood, ruin, and confusion. And of all that Charles Stuart was the root and contriver. But Cromwell was not only a Puritan, saturated with Biblical canons of morality and justice: he was also a profound statesman. He had struggled, against hope and inclination, for a monarchic settlement of the errand dispute. Slowly he had come to know—not only that the man, Charles Stuart, was incurably treacherous, but that any settlement of Parliament with the old Feudal Monarchy was impossible. As the head of the king rolled on the scaffold the old Feudal Monarchy expired for ever. In January 1649 a great mark was set in the course of the national life—the Old Rule behind it, the New Rule before it. Parliamentary government, the consent of the nation, equality of rights, and equity in the law—all date from this great New Departure. The Stuarts indeed returned for one generation, but with the sting of the Old Monarchy gone, and only to disappear almost without a blow. The Church of England returned; but not the Church of Laud or of Charles. The peers returned, but as a meek House of Lords, with their castles razed, their feudal rights and their political power extinct. It is said that the regicides killed Charles I. only to make Charles II. king. It is not so. They killed the Old Monarchy; and the restored monarch was by no means its heir, but a royal Stadtholder or Hereditary President. In 1649, when Charles I. ceased to live, the true monarchy of England ceased to reign. Oliver Cromwell was for ten years supreme ruler; whilst Charles II. was a despised and forgotten exile. The monarchies, peerages, and churches of the civilised world roared with horror and rage; but in five years the rage was spent, and England was settling into new lines, which might possibly have been permanent, and which certainly prepared her present constitutional system. The solemn judgment of Charles Stuart as a traitor to his people, as a public officer who had criminally abused his trust, gave a new life to the history of England, and ultimately to the modern history of Europe.

CHAPTER VIII

THE CAMPAIGN IN IRELAND

A.D. 1649–1650. AETAT. 50–51

By the execution of the king the whole situation was changed. What had been a rebellion under legal forms became a real revolution; in the room of the Parliament men saw a Council of State; in the room of the monarchy, a Commonwealth; and Cromwell was left the one commanding person on either side.

From the day of Pride's Purge, Parliament was never more than a name, a form; but not a power, or even a reality. Parliament, in truth, had been consumed in the act of bringing the king to trial. When the House of Peers was abolished, and the Commonwealth proclaimed, the constitution was obviously at an end. In appointing the Council of State, the House of Commons (or rather the remnant of it which still sat) formally transferred the functions it had wielded for more than eight years to a council which was really a joint-committee of itself and the army. Such a committee was a necessity; but it obviously rested on a revolutionary basis. It consisted of men prepared for a revolutionary and not a constitutional settlement. And amongst such men Cromwell was plainly supreme. Thus, from the day when the king's head fell at Whitehall until the day of his own death there, nearly ten years later, Cromwell was the acknowledged master of England.

It is in vain to repeat that the execution of the king was a mere act of vengeance, a blunder which substituted a young and popular prince for his deposed father. However it be judged, it was at once the symbol and the cause of a profound revolution. The instinct of the army from the first fastened on it as the only guarantee that their work should be a permanent revolution and not a passing insurrection; and slowly the judgment of Cromwell was forced to adopt it in that sense. The sentence upon Charles was the end of the Feudal Monarchy and of all its attributes. It also virtually set aside at once Constitution and Parliament. It compelled the nation to look for a new settlement under new men. Above all, it made a personal ruler the great necessity of the hour. The king being dead, the throne itself destroyed, and the three Estates of the Realm suppressed, a dictator became inevitable. And there was but one possible dictator.

In the formation of the Council of State, in the compromise by which Republicans, like Vane and Fairfax, opposed to regicide were reconciled to take their place in it, in the careful reorganisation of the whole administrative and legal service, the directing spirit of Cromwell is traceable, though, after the first sittings, he had no official supremacy. The House, indeed, rejected Ireton and Harrison from the council, either as Cromwell's men or as too violent revolutionists. In the words of Capel to Cromwell before the king's death, he was the figure which gave its denomination to the cyphers that followed. The organisation of government through the Council of State, the execution of the Duke of Hamilton and the other Royalist prisoners, the rigorous enforcement of the Republican style, were all measures which had Cromwell's support, if they were not due to his influence.

The condition of England without was, however, for the moment more pressing even than her condition within. The new Republic was not recognised by foreign sovereigns. Its enemies were upheld, and its agents were insulted throughout Europe. The bond that had held together the three kingdoms was dissolved. Scotland proclaimed Prince Charles as king. The contending factions in Ireland were at last united by the execution of Charles; Rupert was there with a fleet; and except for a few hard-pressed garrisons, Ireland was now an independent and hostile country.

The reconquest of Ireland was by all felt to be the most urgent interest of the young Commonwealth; there was almost as much agreement to entrust Cromwell with the task; and after some consideration, and prayerful consultations in the army, he accepted the duty. The condition of England was precarious indeed; service in Ireland was not popular in the army; and an ambitious adventurer would have been loath to quit England whilst the first place was still unoccupied. It was at great risk to the cause, and at much personal sacrifice, that Cromwell accepted the difficult post in Ireland as his first duty to his country and to religion. His campaign and the subsequent settlement in Ireland are amongst those things which weigh heaviest on Cromwell's memory, and which of his stoutest admirers one only has heartily approved. Fortunately, there is no part of his policy where his conduct is more simple and his motives are more plain. The Irish policy of Cromwell was the traditional policy of all Englishmen of his creed and party, and was distinguished from theirs only by his personal vigour and thoroughness. He was neither better nor worse than the English Puritans, or rather all English statesmen for many generations: he was only keener and stronger. When he, with Vane, Fairfax, Whitelocke, and other commissioners., went to the Guildhall to obtain a loan for the campaign, they told the Common Council that this was a struggle not between Independent and Presbyterian, but between Papist and Protestant; that Papacy or Popery were not to be endured in that kingdom; and they cited the maxim of James I.: "Plant Ireland with Puritans, root out Papists, and then secure it."

To Cromwell, as to all English Puritans, it seemed a self-evident truth that one of the three realms could not be suffered to become Catholic; as little could it be suffered to become independent, or the open practice of the Catholic religion allowed there, any more than in England; finally, that peace and prosperity could never be secured in Ireland without a dominant and preponderating order of English birth and Protestant belief. By Cromwell, as by the whole Puritan body—we may fairly say by the whole body of Protestants—the Irish Rebellion of 1641 was believed to have opened with a barbarous, treacherous, and wholesale massacre, followed during nine years by one prolonged scene of confusion and bloodshed, ending in an almost complete extinction of the Protestant faith and English interests. The victorious party, and Cromwell more deeply than others, entered on the recovery of Ireland in the spirit of a religious war, to restore to the Protestant cause one of the three realms, which had revolted to the powers of darkness. Such was for centuries the spirit of Protestant England.

The preparations for the reconquest of Ireland were all taken on a large and careful scale. But a pressing danger had first to be dealt with. The individualist doctrines of Independency and the prayer-meetings of the army had led to their natural issue—an outburst of democratic fanaticism; and democratic fanaticism in the army could only end in mutiny. It would have been difficult for Cromwell to reconcile in theory his own teaching in the troopers' prayer-meetings with rigid discipline, and with unfaltering submission to the authority of the council. But Cromwell was never at any time troubled with the need of making his theories consistent. "I tell you, sir," he said in the council about the Levellers, "you have no other way to deal with these men but to break them to pieces, or they will break us." He instinctively felt that a general mutiny in the army was ruin to his cause.

His own action was a model of swiftness, energy, and

severity, mixed with moderation, and even sympathy. In the three chief outbursts—in the city, in Hyde Park, in Oxfordshire—he is the same man. By lightning rapidity of movement, by instant decision of purpose, by terrible sternness in punishing, with complete control of temper, with inflexible hold on the paramount authority of general and Parliament—in turn he orders, harangues, argues, preaches, and implores, appealing at once to the soldiers' sense of discipline, their religion, their patriotism, and their fear of the Provost-Marshal. In the end, he convinces the heart rather than overawes the spirit. The famous scene in the churchyard at Burford is one of the most impressive and dramatic of the whole war: the ringleaders are drawn out for execution; three are shot, then the slaughter is stayed, the Lieutenant-General rises in the pulpit, and pours out such a homily, that with tears and groans the mutinous troopers return to duty. In suppressing mutiny, Cromwell is always at his best, and reminds us of Caesar or Germanicus with the legionaries. And in this great crisis—one of the most dangerous that the Commonwealth passed—but four lives were taken by the Provost-Marshal.

Five months were occupied in the preparations for this distant and difficult campaign. Cromwell's nomination was on the 15th of March. On the same day Milton was appointed Latin Secretary to the Council. During April Cromwell arranged the marriage of his eldest son with the daughter of a very quiet, unambitious squire. On the 10th of July he set forth from London with much military state. His lifeguard was a body of gentlemen "as is hardly to be paralleled in the world." He still waited a month in the west, his wife and family around him; and thence wrote his beautiful letter to Mayor about his son, and the letter to "my beloved daughter Dorothy Cromwell, at Hursley." At length all was ready, and he set sail on the 13th of August, with 9000 men in about 100 ships. He was invested with supreme civil, as well as military, command in Ireland; amply supplied with material, and a fleet. Ireton, his son-in-law, was his second in command.

On landing in Dublin, the general made a speech to the people, in which he spoke of his purpose as "the great work against the barbarous and bloodthirsty Irish, and all their adherents and confederates, for the propagating of the Gospel of Christ, the establishing of truth and peace, and restoring that bleeding nation to its former happiness and tranquillity." His first act was to remodel the Irish army, making "a huge purge of the army which we found here: it was an army made up of dissolute and debauched men"; and the general issued a proclamation against swearing and drunkenness, and another against the "wickedness" that had been taken by the soldiery "to abuse, rob, and pillage, and too often to execute cruelties upon the country people," promising to protect all peaceable inhabitants, and to pay them in ready money for all goods. Two soldiers were shortly hanged for disobeying these orders. Having made a general muster of his forces in Dublin, and formed a complete body of 15,000 horse and foot, he selected a force of 10,000 stout, resolute men, and advanced on Drogheda (in English, Tredagh). Drogheda is a seaport town on the Boyne, about twenty-three miles due north of Dublin. It was strongly fortified, and Ormond, as Clarendon tells us, had put into it "the flower of his army, both of soldiers and officers, *most of them English*, to the number of 3000 foot, and two or three good troops of horse, provided with all things." Sir Arthur Ashton, an English Catholic, an officer "of great name and experience, and who at that time made little doubt of defending it against all the power of Cromwell," was in chief command.

Cromwell's horse reached Drogheda on 3rd September, his memorable day; some skirmishes followed, and on the 10th the batteries opened in earnest, after formal summons to the garrison to surrender. A steeple and a tower were beaten down the first day; all through the 11th the batteries continued, and at length effected "two reasonable breaches." About five in the evening of the second day the storm began. "After some hot dispute we entered, about seven or eight hundred men; the enemy disputing it very stiffly with us." But a tremendous rally of the garrison—wherein Colonel Castle and other officers were killed—drove out the column, which retreated disheartened and baffled. Then the general did that which as commander he was seldom wont to do, and which he passes in silence in his despatches. "Resolved," says Ludlow, "to put all upon it, he went down to the breach; and calling out a fresh reserve of Colonel Ewer's men, he put himself at their head, and with the word 'our Lord God,' led them up again with courage and resolution, though they met with a hot dispute." Thus encouraged to recover their loss, they got ground of the enemy, forced him to quit his entrenchments, and poured into the town. There many retreated to the Millmount, a place very strong and difficult of access; "exceedingly high and strongly palisadoed." This place commanded the whole town: thither Sir Arthur Ashton and other important officers had betaken themselves. But the storming party burst in, and were ordered by Cromwell to put them all to the sword. The rest of the garrison fled over the bridge to the northern side of the town; but the Ironsides followed them hotly, both horse and foot, and drove them into St. Peter's Church and the towers of the ramparts. St. Peter's Church was set on fire by Cromwell's order. He writes to the speaker: "Indeed, being in the heat of action, I forbade them to spare any that were in arms in the Town: and I think that night they put to the sword about 2000 men." Next day the other towers were summoned, and the work of slaughter was renewed for two days, until the entire garrison was annihilated. It was unquestionably a massacre. "That night they put to the sword about 2000 men." In Peter's Church "near 1000 of them were put to the sword, fleeing thither for safety." "Their friars were knocked on the head promiscuously." "I do not think we lost 100 men upon the place." Such are passages from Cromwell's own despatches.

The slaughter was indeed prodigious. The general writes: "I believe we put to the sword the whole number of the defendants. I do not think Thirty of the whole number escaped with their lives." "The enemy were about 3000 strong in the town." "I do not believe, neither do I hear, that any officer escaped with his life, save only one Lieutenant." He subsequently gives a detailed list of the slain, amounting to about 3000. Hugh Peters, the chaplain, reports as follows: "Sir, the truth is, Drogheda is taken, 3552 of the enemy slain, and 64 of ours. Ashton, the governor, killed, none spared." It is also certain that quarter was refused. "I forbade them to spare any that were in arms in the town." It is expressly told us that all officers and all priests taken were killed. From the days of Clarendon it has been repeated by historians that men, women, and children were indiscriminately slaughtered, and there is evidence of an eye-witness to that effect; but this is not believed to have been done by the order or even with the knowledge of the general. The Royalist accounts insist that quarter was promised at first; and that the butchery of men in cold blood was carried on for days. Here again the act must have been exceptional and without authority.[1]

To Cromwell himself this fearful slaughter was a signal triumph of the truth. "It hath pleased God to bless our endeavours." "This hath been a marvellous great mercy." "I am persuaded that this is a righteous judgment of God upon these barbarous wretches, who have imbued their hands in so much innocent blood; and that it will tend to prevent the effusion of blood for the future. Which are the satisfactory grounds to such actions; which otherwise cannot but work remorse and regret." "It was set upon some of our hearts, That a great thing should be done, not by power

1 [See Appendix C.]

or might, but by the Spirit of God." In the same sense it was received by Parliament and Council of State, by some of the noblest spirits of their age. Ludlow says simply that this "extraordinary severity was used to discourage others from making opposition." It had always been the policy of Cromwell in battle to inflict a crushing defeat; at Marston, at Naseby, and at Preston he had "taken execution of the enemy" for hours and over miles of country. At Basing and elsewhere, after a summons and a storm, he had slaughtered hundreds without mercy. And such was the law of war in that age, practised on both sides without hesitation. But the item of numbers and of time tells very heavily here. The killing of hundreds in hot blood differs from the massacre of thousands during days. There was no such act in the whole Civil War as the massacre—prolonged for days—of 3000 men enclosed in walls entirely at the mercy of their captors, to say nothing of the promiscuous slaughter of priests, if not of women and unarmed men. In England such a deed could not have been done; and not in Ireland, but that they were Catholics fighting in defence of their faith. The fact that the garrison were Catholics, fighting on Irish soil, placed them, to the Puritan Englishman, out of the pale. No admiration for Cromwell, for his genius, courage, and earnestness—no sympathy with the cause that he upheld in England—can blind us to the truth, that the lurid light of this great crime burns still after centuries across the history of England and of Ireland; that it is one of those damning charges which the Puritan theology has yet to answer at the bar of humanity.

The tremendous blow at Drogheda struck terror into Ormond's forces. Dundalk and Trim were abandoned in haste. O'Neil swore a great oath that as Cromwell had stormed Drogheda, if he should storm hell he should take it. One fort after another yielded; and in a fortnight from the taking of Drogheda, Cromwell was master of the country north of Dublin. Marching from Dublin south, on the 23rd of September, his army took forts in Wicklow, Arklow, and Enniscorthy; and on the 1st of October the general encamped before Wexford, an important seaport at the south-eastern corner of the island. The town was strong, with a rampart 15 feet thick, a garrison of over 2000 men, 100 cannon, and in the harbour two ships armed with 54 guns. Cromwell summoned the governor to surrender, not obscurely threatening him with the fate of Drogheda.

"It will clearly appear," he said, "where the guilt will lie, if innocent persons should come to suffer with the nocent." His terms were quarter and prison to the officers, quarter and freedom to the soldiers, protection from plunder to the town. These terms were refused, and both sides continued the fight. Suddenly, some breaches being made in the castle, the captain surrendered it, and by a surprise the whole army of the Commonwealth poured into the town. The townsmen took part in the defence; and townsmen and garrison together were forced into the market-place. There, as at Drogheda, a promiscuous massacre ensued. Upwards of 2000 were slain, and with them not a few of the citizens; and the town was delivered over to pillage. It is asserted by the Catholic writers that a body of women, who had taken refuge round the cross, were deliberately slaughtered, and that a general massacre took place without regard to sex or age. Priests were killed at once, and in the sack and pillage, undoubtedly some non-combatants, it may be some women and children. But these things were incidents of such a storm, and were not done by design or order of the general. This is his own story:

> "Whilst I was preparing of it; studying to preserve the Town from plunder, that it might be of the more use to you and your Army,—the Captain, who was one of the Commissioners, being fairly treated, yielded up the Castle to us. Upon the top of which our men no sooner appeared, but the Enemy quitted the Walls of the Town; which our men perceiving, ran violently upon the Town with their ladders, and stormed it. And when they were come into

> the marketplace, the Enemy making a stiff resistance, our forces brake them; and then put all to the sword that came in their way. Two boatfuls of the Enemy attempting to escape, being over- prest with numbers, sank; whereby were drowned near three-hundred of them. I believe, in all, there was lost of the Enemy not many less than Two-thousand; and I believe not Twenty of yours from first to last of the Siege. And indeed it hath, not without cause, been deeply set upon our hearts, That, we intending better to this place than so great a ruin, hoping the Town might be of more use to you and your Army, yet God would not have it so; but by an unexpected providence, in His righteous justice, brought a just judgment upon them; causing them to become a prey to the Soldier—who in their piracies had made preys of so many families, and now with their bloods to answer the cruelties which they have exercised upon the lives of divers poor Protestants! . . .
>
> "This Town is now so in your power, that of the former inhabitants, I believe scarce one in twenty can challenge any property in their houses. Most of them are run away, and many of them killed in this service. And it were to be wished that an honest people would come and plant here."

The blow that had desolated Drogheda and Wexford did not need to be repeated. Ross was taken; the Munster garrisons—Cork, Kinsale, and others—joined the Commonwealth. And within three months of Cromwell's march from Dublin, the whole of the towns on the eastern and southern sides of Ireland, except Waterford and some others, were reduced to the Parliament. Waterford resisted him; a wet winter set in; and with the wet, dysentery and fever. Cromwell fell ill; many officers sickened; General Jones died. "What England lost hereby is above me to speak," wrote the general. "I am sure I lost a noble friend and companion in labours. You see how God mingles out the cup to us. Indeed we are at this time a crazy company: yet we live in His sight; and shall work the time that is appointed us, and shall rest after that in peace."

After a short rest, on the 29th of January, Cromwell was again in the field. He passed into the heart of the island—into Kilkenny and Tipperary; Clogheen, Castletown, Fethard, Callan, Cashel, Cahir, Kilkenny, Carrick, were taken after a short defence; and Clonmel at last surrendered after a desperate attempt at storm, which cost Cromwell, it is said, 2000 men. This was his last great fight in Ireland. He had now crushed opposition in the whole east and south of the island; the north had returned to the Protestant cause; Waterford fell soon after; and except Limerick, Galway, and a few fortresses, the Parliament's forces were masters of the island. Cromwell had been nine months in Ireland, and at no time possessed an army of more than 15,000 men. Within that time he had taken a score of strong places, and in a series of bloody encounters had dispersed or annihilated armies of far greater number than his own. An official summons to England had been sent in January; it was not till the end of May that he actually obeyed it.

As Cromwell's practice in warfare in Ireland differed somewhat from what he observed elsewhere, and as from that day to this it has been the subject of furious invective, a few words thereon are plainly needed. Cromwell had gone to Ireland, at imminent risk to his cause, to recover it to the Parliament in the shortest possible time, and with a relatively small army. He had gone there first to punish (as was believed) a wholesale massacre and a social revolution, to restore the Irish soil to England, and to replace the Protestant ascendancy. In the view of the Commonwealth government, the mass was by law a crime, Catholic priests were legally outlaws, and all who resisted the Parliament were constructively guilty of murder and rebellion. Such were the accepted axioms of the whole Puritan party, and of Cromwell as much as any man.

In such a war he held that where a place was stormed after summons, all in arms might justly be put to the sword, though no longer capable of resistance, and though they amounted to thousands. "They," he writes, "refusing conditions seasonably offered, were all put to the sword." Repeatedly he shot all officers who surrendered at discretion. Officers who had once served the Parliament he hanged. Priests, taken alive, were hanged. "As for your clergymen, as you call them," wrote Oliver to the Governor of Kilkenny, "in case you agree for a surrender, they shall march away safely; but if they fall otherwise into my hands, I believe they know what to expect from me." At Gowran the castle surrendered. "The next day, the Colonel, the Major, and the rest of the Commission officers were shot to death: . . . In the same castle also he took a Popish Priest, who was chaplain to the Catholics in this regiment; who was caused to be hanged." The Bishop of Ross, marching to save Clonmel with 5000 men, was defeated by Broghill, captured, and hanged in sight of his own men. The Bishop of Clogher was routed by Coote and Venables and shared the same fate. "All their friars were knocked on the head promiscuously," Cromwell wrote at Drogheda, as the Catholic martyrologies assert with torture. Peaceable inhabitants were not to be molested. But all who had taken part in or supported the rebellion of 1641 were liable to justice.

For soldiers he found a new career. By a stroke of profound policy he encouraged foreign embassies to enlist Irish volunteers, giving them a free pass abroad. And thus it is said some 40,000 Irishmen ultimately passed into the service of foreign sovereigns. With great energy and skill the Lord-Lieutenant set about the reorganisation of government in Ireland. A leading feature of this was the Cromwellian settlement afterwards carried out under the Protectorate, by which immense tracts of land in the provinces of Ulster, Leinster, and Munster were allotted to English settlers, and the landowners of Irish birth removed into Connaught.

Cromwell has left on record his own principles of action in the famous Declaration which he issued in January in reply to the Irish bishops:

> Ireland, he says, was once united to England. Englishmen had inheritances and leases which they had purchased: and they lived peaceably. "You broke this Union. You, unprovoked, put the English to the most unheard-of and most barbarous massacre (without respect of sex or age) that ever the sun beheld." It is a fig-leaf of pretence, that they fight for their king: really it is for men guilty of blood:— *bellum prelaticum et religiosum*—as you say. "You are a part of Anti-Christ, whose kingdom the Scripture so expressly speaks should be laid in blood, yea in the blood of the saints." "You quote my own words at Ross," he says, "that where the Parliament of England have power, the exercise of the mass will not be allowed of; and you say that this is a design to extirpate the Catholic religion. I cannot extirpate what has never been rooted. These are my intentions. I shall not, where I have power, suffer the exercise of the mass. Nor shall I suffer any Papists, where I find them seducing the people, or by overt act violating the laws." "As for the people, what thoughts they have in matters of religion in their own breasts I cannot reach." But as to the charge of massacre, destruction, or banishment he says: "*Give us an instance of one man since my coming into Ireland, not in arms, massacred, destroyed or banished; concerning the massacre or the destruction of whom justice hath not been done, or endeavoured to be done.*"

This very pointed and daring challenge could hardly have been publicly made by such a man as Cromwell, if, to his knowledge, a slaughter of women and unarmed men had occurred. On the other hand, it is certain that priests and others had been killed in cold blood; and a general who delivers over a city to pillage, and forbids quarter, can hardly say where outrage and massacre will cease. As to banishment, the "Cromwellian settlement" was necessarily based on the banishment of those whom the settlers displaced.

With regard to the policy of confiscation and resettlement, Cromwell warmly justifies it. It is the just way of meeting rebellion, he says. You have forfeited your estates, and it is just to raise money by escheating your lands. But apart from the land forfeited, which is but a part of the account, if ever men were engaged in a just and righteous cause it was this, he asserts:

> "We are come to ask an account of the innocent blood that hath been shed; and to endeavour to bring to an account,—by the presence and blessing of the Almighty, in whom alone is our hope and strength,—all who, by appearing in arms, seek to justify the same. We come to break the power of lawless Rebels, who having cast off the Authority of England, live as enemies to Human Society; whose principles, the world hath experience, are, To destroy and subjugate all men not complying with them. We come, by the assistance of God, to hold forth and maintain the lustre and glory of English Liberty in a Nation where we have an undoubted right to do it;—wherein the people of Ireland (if they listen not to such seducers as you are) may equally participate in all benefits; to rise liberty and fortune equally with Englishmen, if they keep out of arms."

Such was the basis of the famous "Cromwellian settlement"—by far the most thorough act in the long history of the conquest of Ireland; by far the most wholesale effort to impose on Ireland the Protestant faith and English ascendancy. Wholesale and thorough, but not enough for its purpose. It failed like all the others; did more, perhaps, than any other to bind Ireland to the Catholic Church, and to alienate Irishmen from the English rule. On the Irish race it has left undying memories and a legend of tyranny which is summed up in the peasants' saying of the *Curse of Cromwell.*

Cromwell, not worse than the Puritans and English of his age, but nobler and more just, must yet for generations to come bear the weight of the legendary "curse." He was the incarnation of Puritan passion, the instrument of English ambition; the official authority by whom the whole work was carried out, the one man ultimately responsible for the rest; and it is thus that on him lies chiefly the weight of this secular national quarrel.

Oliver, leaving Ireland to his son-in-law Ireton, and appointing civil and military chiefs, reached London on the 31st of May. Here he was received with a salute of big guns, honours, and acclamations; Fairfax, members of Parliament, and a great multitude coming out to welcome him. The Cockpit was appointed as his residence; the city of London, Parliament, and many persons of quality offered their congratulations "on the safe arrival of his Excellence after so many dangers both by sea and land, wherein God had preserved him, and the wonderful successes which He had given him." As he passed Tyburn in his thronged procession, one said to him, "See what a multitude of people come to attend your triumph!" He answered with a smile and very unconcerned, "*More would come to see me hanged!*"

Appendix C

No part of the history of these times is more beset with contradictory accounts than the details of the Irish war. Race hatred and sectarian mendacity have carried contradiction to the extreme limit. Was the garrison of Drogheda English or Irish; was there a promiscuous massacre there of citizens and women? On these two points there is deliberate contradiction.

As to the garrison, Clarendon says, "most of them English." In another place he speaks of the "massacre of that body of English at Tredagh." So also say Ludlow and Bates. Whitelocke says, "mostly Irish." Ormond says they were chiefly Catholics; and the Irish writers interpret this to mean Irish. Cromwell's despatch at Drogheda ends thus: "2500 Foot-soldiers besides Staff-officers, Surgeons, etc." This appears in the *Parliamentary History* with the added words, "*and many inhabitants*," and has been so copied into many histories.

The letter from Clonmel in *Cromwelliana* (10th May 1650)

runs thus: "We discovered the enemy to be gone, and very early this morning pursued them, and fell upon their reare of straglers, and killed above 200, *besides those we slew in the storm*." S. Dillingham, writing to Sancroft from Gutter Lane (May 1650), evidently reporting this news, relates it thus: "They were mad when they came in, and sending to pursue, *cut off two hundred women and children!*" (Cary, ii. 218). The Rev. Denis Murphy, S.J., in his *Cromwell in Ireland* cites this passage, but alters "they paid dear" into "we paid dear," as if from an eye-witness.

Parliament voted "that the House doth approve the execution done at Drogheda, as an act both of justice to them and mercy to others who may be warned by it; and that the Council of State prepare a letter to be signed by the Speaker." Ludlow, Fairfax, Col. Hutchinson, Vane, Whitelocke, were members of the Council of State; Milton was its Secretary; Fairfax was Commander-in-Chief. Milton writes in his panegyric (*Defensio Secunda*): "*Tu, uno statim praelio Hibernicorum opes fregisti*." Lucy Hutchinson calmly mentions "how Cromwell finished the conquest of Ireland," and seems to see in it only the hand of God.

CHAPTER IX

THE CAMPAIGN IN SCOTLAND – WORCESTER

A.D. 1650–1651. AETAT. 51–52

War between England and Scotland had long been imminent. When Cromwell returned from Ireland it became his immediate task. In June Charles landed in Scotland, and was proclaimed there king of the three kingdoms. The Kirk party which had defeated Montrose determined to support the Stuart on his taking the Covenant. They collected an army on the border, and inflamed the Scotch people against the Commonwealth. Underneath the ancient national quarrel lay the yet deeper quarrel of religion. The dominant party in Scotland were fanatical partisans of the most rigid form of Presbyterian orthodoxy. The chiefs of the English Commonwealth, who had suppressed Presbyterianism and monarchy together, were no less resolute to found a Bible freedom of Independency.

It is now useless to discuss whether the Scotch had given just cause for war; whether war between the two countries could be avoided by wisdom and moderation. Fairfax doubted if it were just, and the famous deputation which Cromwell headed failed to shake him. We officers, said the Lord-Lieutenant, desire to serve under no other general. The Scotch have invaded us once, and give good cause to think they intend another invasion. War between us is unavoidable. Is it better to have this war in the bowels of another country or in our own? Cromwell was certainly in earnest; but no arguments could shake Fairfax; he resigned his commission, and never again took part in public affairs. The next day Cromwell was appointed Commander-in-Chief of all the forces raised and to be raised by authority of Parliament. Three days later he set out for the north, where an army of some 16,000 men had for some time been mustering.

The sudden advance of Cromwell, fresh from the bloody campaign in Ireland, struck dismay into the Scotch border. The preachers inveighed against him as a blasphemer, leading an army of plunderers and murderers. The country was laid bare and the male inhabitants withdrawn from the border up to Edinburgh. David Lesley, Cromwell's old comrade at Marston, a thorough soldier, trained in the wars of Gustavus, was put in command; his plan of campaign was to wear out the invader by avoiding battle, and cutting off his supplies. The English general crossed the border on 22nd July, and advanced somewhat slowly along the coast, resting on his ships. The sternest discipline was enforced. Then began a long and characteristic duel of manifestoes and declarations, issued by the chiefs and preachers in each army. Both sides, with abundant quotations from Scripture, insisted that God was on their side. The Scotch maintained that the Commonwealth had broken the Covenant. The Cromwellians retorted that the Scotch Presbyterians were laying the seeds of perpetual war by taking their grand enemy to their bosoms, and by engaging to restore him to his throne in England and Ireland. It was not so much a battle between two armies, as between two rival congregations in arms. Both sides intensely believed that God was with them, and His Word gave clear assurance that all their opponents should be utterly cast down. Never was national and religious animosity more fiercely kindled amongst men who had so much in common, and who were implicitly guided by the same Book. It was a religious war between two sects, each of which regarded the other as schismatics. Thus the English army entered Scotland consumed with zeal to fight it out to the last man in defence of the Commonwealth, and "to live and die with their renowned general."

Some indecisive actions followed, where the great superiority of the English soldiers was manifest, and especially their strength in horse. Lesley doggedly refused battle, and fell back to a line resting on the coast between Edinburgh and Leith, with some 22,000 men. All through August Cromwell strove to force Lesley to a battle; but "he lay very strong," and could not be attacked in his positions. The weather was wet and stormy; provisions were failing; sickness disabled a tenth of the men; and the situation became indeed grave. From side to side the English general attempted to cut off the Scotch from their supplies, but the whole north and north-west lay open to them; Cromwell could not advance far from his base on the coast, and the ships could not lie in the Forth.

Unable to force the enemy to battle, he again betook himself to spiritual arms, and issued those two amazing appeals—one to the Kirk and the other to their general. As in the midst of his Irish campaign he passionately inveighed against the Irish bishops, so now, invader in arms as he was, he laboriously argued with the godly men of the Kirk as with brothers in the Lord. "I beseech you, in the bowels of Christ, think it possible you may be mistaken." Are you sure, he argues, that this your league with wicked and carnal men is a covenant of God? "I pray you read the twenty-eighth of Isaiah, from the fifth to the fifteenth verse. And do not scorn to know that it is the Spirit that quickens and giveth life." And to General Lesley he writes: "That under pretence of the Covenant, a king should be taken in by you, to be imposed upon us"—a king who now has a Popish army fighting for and under him in Ireland, and who is surrounded by Malignants fighting and plotting for him in England

and elsewhere. It does not appear that either side designed these declarations for their own men more than the enemy. Both profoundly believed their own cause; and if they did not think they could persuade the other, they could not understand how godly men could resist truth so plain and Scriptural.

Twice had Cromwell advanced upon the enemy, and twice he had retired baffled. His men were weary with marching, exhausted by the wet and storms, ill-fed, and reduced by disease, when, sullenly fighting, they fell back on Dunbar, 1st September. By a very skilful manoeuvre Lesley passed his whole army round the retreating invader, planted himself to the south of him securely on the Lammermuir Hills, and occupied with a strong guard the pass which was the key of the road to England. Cromwell's position was now very critical. He had scarcely 11,000 men left under arms: and these, as one of them wrote, "a poor, scattered, hungry, discouraged army." The enemy, just double his number, was placed on a strong range of hills between him and his own country, and had occupied the only road by the sea along which he could retreat across the border. His whole force lay on a small promontory jutting out into the Northern Sea, with no other base than his ships. He saw the danger fully; and on the 2nd of September he wrote thus privately to warn Sir Arthur Haselrig, the Governor of Newcastle:

> "We are upon, an engagement very difficult. The enemy hath blocked up our way at the pass at Cockburnspath, through which we cannot get almost without a miracle. He lieth so upon the hills that we know not how to come that way without great difficulty; and our lying here daily consumeth our men, who fall sick beyond imagination."
> Then he warns the governor to provide against a catastrophe, to get together what forces he can, to send to friends in the south, to inform Sir H. Vane, but not to make it public. "Whatever becomes of us, it will be well for you to get what forces you can together; and the south to help

> what they can. The business nearly concerneth all good people." But he goes on: "All shall work for good. Our spirits are comfortable, praised be the Lord! though our present condition be as it is."

With such foresight Oliver faced a great peril, that it might not lead to the ruin of the Commonwealth. As Harvey, one of his attendants, writes: "He was a strong man, in the dark perils of war, in the high places of the field; hope shone in him like a pillar of fire, when it had gone out in all the others."

Cromwell's position was "very difficult," as he said, but not desperate. He was not yet driven to embark either men or guns. A battle would give him victory; and one mistake of the enemy would secure him his battle. That mistake at last Lesley made. Either forced by the Kirk committee and the influence of the preachers over his men, or urged on to crush the invader at one blow, he began to draw down his army towards the shore. That very afternoon, 2nd September, Cromwell, walking with Lambert, noticed the change of position; how the enemy's right wing had descended into the plain. "The Lord hath delivered them into our hand!" was the cry of Cromwell, as vague tradition relates. This he thought, if he did not utter the words; Lambert and Monk were of the same mind, and so were other officers. That night a plan of battle was drawn up, the formations made, and leaders were chosen for each line. Lesley had drawn down his wing to the coast, hoping to surround and crush the English, in the act, as he supposed, of embarking his men. Cromwell's design was to hold the main Scotch army with his big guns, whilst he fell suddenly with his best troops on Lesley's right wing, and so to roll it back upon its centre. The night was wild and wet; the moon covered with clouds. The English lay partly in tents; the Scotch on the open hillside, crouched for shelter in the soaked shocks of corn. Both armies rested beside their arms, waiting eagerly for dawn; and on both sides many gathered in companies, and prayed aloud and for the last time to the God of Battles.

At four in the morning by the light of the moon the English began to move. Two hours were spent in the sodden fields in completing their formation. Then they advanced to the charge with the word that day: *The Lord of Hosts.* For some time the dispute was hot and stiff. The cannons roared against the main line of the Scotch army, still posted on its hill, and unable to deploy freely across the brook and ravine in their front. At first their right wing in the plain drove back the English troopers across the brook, where it opens out towards the sea. But, supported by the foot which now advanced, and aided by Cromwell's favourite resource of a flank charge of cavalry, they returned to the assault and drove back the enemy, both horse and foot. "After the first repulse," runs the general's despatch, "they were made by the Lord of Hosts as stubble to their swords." "The best of the Scotch horse being broken through and through in less than an hour's dispute, their whole army being put to confusion, it became a total rout; our men having the chase and execution of them near eight miles." The right wing of Lesley was alone the free part of his army. It had been outmatched and utterly crushed in less than an hour by Cromwell's main force. Three thousand of the Scotch were cut down in the first onset. "They run! I profess they run!" cried Oliver as he watched the charge. The main body of the Scotch being planted on a hillside, and behind a deep brook that ran in a ravine between them and the enemy, had long been pounded by Cromwell's cannon without being able to deploy. As at last they descended the hill to support their right wing, it dashed in upon them in its flight, the horsemen in panic riding down their supports. The whole army broke and dispersed, flying in all directions: some south, some north.

Just then over the eastern ocean burst the first gleam of the sun through the morning mist. And above the roar of the battle was heard the voice of the general: "Let God arise, let his enemies be scattered." Then, as the whole Scotch army fled in wild confusion, "the Lord- General made a halt," steadying his men and firing them afresh for the pursuit: he sang the 117th Psalm: "O praise the Lord, all ye nations: praise him, all ye people. For his merciful kindness is great towards us: and the truth of the Lord endureth for ever. Praise ye the Lord."

Such was Dunbar battle on Cromwell's great day. The overthrow had been complete. Three thousand dead lay on the field; thousands fell in the chase; 10,000 prisoners were taken; the whole baggage and train, all the artillery, great and small; 15,000 stand of arms, 200 colours. On the part of the victors, but two officers and twenty men had fallen. It is seldom that war sees a victory so rapid, so overwhelming, and so wholly one-sided.

The Scotch were brave and hardy soldiers, adequately equipped, fired with religious enthusiasm, and twice as numerous as the English. They were at home, resting on their capital, well provisioned, and led by a very experienced soldier, who had baffled Cromwell for six weeks. But the bulk of their men were raw, unorganised levies; the great majority of the officers were without any training, and the preachers had far more authority than the officers. The Scotch host was rather a church than an army. Cromwell's army from first to last was a perfect body of warriors—generals, officers, horse, and foot; unsurpassed in courage, skill in arms, in discipline, and in *morale*. The campaign had been one to try the best troops; and they had never wavered before disease, hunger, or fatigue. Cromwell, if not one of the great masters of strategy, was certainly a consummate leader on the field of battle. His tactics on the day of Dunbar were as complete as those of Lesley were faulty. His men were troops never surpassed as soldiers, stirred with the energy of martyrs: they were led that day with all the insight and the swoop that mark a great commander.

It is another and more complex question whether

Cromwell had shown strategic skill in the campaign. Till the day of Dunbar his campaign had been barely a success. He had no base but his ships, a doubtful resource in such a season and on such a coast; and he made three marches, at least, exposed to singular risk. But before we can judge them to be military blunders we must remember that he was sure of himself—sure of his men. He knew that they were consummate soldiers, facing ill-trained levies. He knew that one hour of battle would decide the campaign, and he acted as so many great generals have acted when, trusting in their own star, and knowing that they led unconquered veterans against a rude militia, they have broken every rule of warfare and plucked victory out of extreme peril. So Hannibal at Cannae, manoeuvring in the plain with a smaller but trained army, had drawn down the larger host of the Romans from their hills, turned suddenly upon them, and crushed them in one awful ruin. There too, till the hour of battle, the victor seemed baffled and hemmed in; there too the defeated army was ruined by pride, self-will, faction, and patriotic rhetoric; and there also it was seen that a great general at the head of a veteran army can outmatch any odds; nay, the courage and enthusiasm of a brave people fighting for their altars and their homes.

The next day Cromwell sent on Lambert to occupy Edinburgh, himself remaining at Dunbar, much embarrassed with his prisoners. Five thousand sick or feeble men he sent away: 5000 others were despatched to England, where they died like flies. That day he wrote to his wife a few words of affection, adding that he was growing an old man, and felt the infirmities of age marvellously stealing upon him. And he found time in the midst of the campaign to write many other letters to his family and friends. Disaster had broken up the Scotch into several parties. The king, with a new army, was holding out in the Highlands, resting on Perth and Stirling. Cromwell, with his generals, occupied the country south of the Forth, and thence to the Clyde.

Long exhortations and wrestlings in spirit, blasts and counter-blasts, passed between the chiefs of the two nations; unceasing efforts were made to reassure the inhabitants; and gradually the bulk of the southern population became accustomed to the firm and moderate rule of Cromwell. On the 1st of January 1651 Charles II. was crowned king at Scone; and gradually withdrawing himself from the Kirk, he gathered an army of the old Loyalist type.

The winter was severe, and Cromwell failed to shake the royal army at Stirling. In one of these expeditions, early in February, the general was seized with his old enemy—ague. He had a severe attack in March 1648; others in Ireland in 1649-50; now a third in less than a year. It fell on him in three successive relapses, endangering his life, breaking his constitution, and paralysing his activity until June. "I thought I should have died of this fit of sickness," he writes to the Council of State, "but the Lord seemeth to dispose otherwise." And to his wife he writes: "In these hopes I wait, and am not without expectation of a gracious return. Pray for me. . . . Truly I am not able as yet to write much. I am weary; and rest, thine." He still, in the intervals of his sickness, marches and gives orders, argues, prays, and preaches, at least as eager to convince as to conquer his misguided Presbyterian brethren. "I shall not need," he writes to the Council, "to recite the extremity of my last sickness: it was so violent that, indeed, my nature was not able to bear the weight thereof. But the Lord was pleased to deliver me, beyond expectation; and to give me cause to say once more, 'He hath plucked me out of the grave!'" So he had written to Fairfax, in his sickness of 1648: "I received in myself the sentence of death, that I might learn to trust in Him that raiseth from the dead, and have no confidence in the flesh. It's a blessed thing to die daily."

His life was saved, but his health was visibly shaken. It was observed that he had grown an old man. And the warning was not lost on him. No portion of his career is more full than is this Scotch campaign of affectionate communings with his family and intimates, meditations on the will of God, and kindly dealing with all with whom he came into personal contact. Cromwell resumed the field in June; and after fruitless attempts to take or surround Stirling, he boldly crossed the Forth into Fife, designing to cut off the Royalist communication. A successful engagement by Lambert, where the Scotch lost 2000 men, gave him a firm hold north of the Forth. He passed across it himself with his main force, and placed himself between Stirling and Perth—which latter surrendered after one day's siege.

The success of Cromwell in his rear, and divisions in his own followers, drove Charles to the desperate adventure with which the long struggle closed. At the end of July he suddenly broke up his camp at Stirling, and made a dash for England by way of Carlisle and the north-western counties. Such an adventure had been talked of and even expected by the Council since the beginning of the year. It was entirely in the reckless spirit of the overweening cavaliers; and Charles had long been withdrawing from the Presbyterians and the politicians to place himself in the hands of the Royalist soldiers. Cromwell heard of the march as he lay before Perth; it is plain with neither surprise nor alarm. There is every reason to believe that he deliberately opened the way for it by marching upon Perth whilst he left the south open. At least, he accepted the alternative either of driving Charles into the western Highlands, or of leaving him free to dash upon his ruin in England. And of the two Cromwell much preferred the last.

The danger was far more apparent than real. It was hardly more serious than the raid of his young kinsman to Derby a hundred years later. There were ample forces to hold and to surround Charles, and little risk of his rousing a new war in England. Cromwell left a garrison in Perth, sent Monk with 6000 men to reduce Stirling and to maintain Scotland, and himself with his main army hastened back across the border by way of Berwick—

> "Resolving," he writes, "to make what speed we can up to the enemy,—who, in his desperation and fear, and out of inevitable necessity, is run to try what he can do this way. I do apprehend that if he goes for England, being some few days' march before us, it will trouble some men's thoughts; and may occasion some inconveniences." He then explains that the present campaign will end the war, and avoid another winter in Scotland. "The Lord," he adds, "will make the desperateness of this counsel of theirs to appear, and the folly of it also. When England was much more unsteady than now; and when a much more considerable army of theirs, unfoiled, invaded you; and we had but a weak force to make resistance at Preston—upon deliberate advice, we chose rather to put ourselves between their army and Scotland: and how that succeeded is not well to be forgotten! This is not out of choice on our part, but by some kind of necessity; and it is to be hoped will have the like issue."

General Harrison, with a strong body of horse on the border, was ordered to hang on the enemy's flank. Lambert, with the main body of the cavalry, was pushed on to follow up his rear. Levies were summoned on many sides, the towns were defended by volunteers, and Cromwell's main army followed with the utmost rapidity.

Charles marched on through Cumberland and Lancashire with a jaded army, some 12,000 strong, summoning towns and calling for recruits; but he met no response. Lord Derby raised a force to join him, but it was cut to pieces by Lilburne; the towns resisted; the country-people flew at his approach, driving off their cattle; Fairfax raised his men in Yorkshire; Colonel Hutchinson in Nottingham; and by the time the king had reached Shropshire, Lambert and Harrison faced him with an equal body of soldiers far better than his own. The Council of State worked night and day with extra-ordinary energy; county militias were everywhere mustering; and Charles, baffled and disheartened, turned to the south-west to Worcester. Here, towards the end of August, Cromwell arrived. He had marched from Perth in little more than three weeks, and found himself in command of more than 30,000 men. Charles was now brought to bay. His men were exhausted by their march in a hostile country, and were circled round with enemies. "We have one stout argument, despair," wrote the Duke of Hamilton; "for we must now either stoutly fight it or die." Cromwell had before him the last cavalier army, which his own troops outnumbered nearly three to one. The Civil War was about to close.

Charles held at Worcester a very strong position. The city was stoutly fortified; it lay on the left or eastern bank of the Severn, a little above the point where the Teme flows into it from the west. A strong fort on a steep hill in advance of the walls defended the city on its south-eastern angle, and a bridge connected it with a suburb on the right, or western, bank of the Severn. Charles posted his main force in the triangle formed by the two rivers, using the city and its outworks as a powerful *tête-de-pont*, or entrenched camp, whence, behind strong walls and on the inner line, his troops could quickly operate, now on the right, now on the left side of the Severn. He broke up the bridge over the Severn at Upton lower down, and occupied in force the bridge over the Terne. There, *à-cheval* on two rivers, and in the triangle between them, the Royalist army stood at bay.

Cromwell appeared before Worcester on the 28th of August. Having an overwhelming force, he was able to divide his army in two sections, and to attack on both sides of the Severn with two forces, each outnumbering the enemy. He himself fortified the hill on the eastern side of the river, and from his batteries cannonaded the city. Fleetwood was despatched down the Severn, which, with great spirit, he crossed on the broken bridge, wounded Massey, the Royalist general, drove back the Scotch on to the Teme, and planted himself firmly on the western bank of the Severn. From the 28th of August till 3rd of September the batteries played on the city, the works drawing closer round it, and the besieged continually giving ground. At dawn on the 3rd of September—his fortunate day—Cromwell ordered his final assault. "This day twelvemonth," runs a despatch, "was glorious at Dunbar, this day hath been glorious at Worcester. The word then was '*The Lord of Hosts*' and so it was now; and indeed the Lord of Hosts was wonderfully with us."

Fleetwood began the day with assailing the Scots on the Teme, Cromwell aiding with a force from the other bank, and between them they succeeded in building two bridges of boats close together; one across Severn, the other across Teme. The triangle thus lost its two river defences. Fleetwood poured into it across the Teme from Upton, and Cromwell, heading the van in person, poured into it across the Severn. The Scotch were driven back from one defence to another, fighting desperately; but they had been taken in flank, and were completely overpowered by the forces converging upon them from both armies. The king, who watched the fight from the tower of the Cathedral, hastily withdrew his men across Severn bridge into the city; and at once commenced a skilful and vigorous manoeuvre. It was now afternoon: the city was still unbroken, and a large part of the Royalist army was safe behind its walls. Suddenly dashing out from the south-eastern gates upon the remnant of Cromwell's army left on the left bank of the Severn, Charles, at the head of his cavalry, broke a regiment of foot and began to force back the weakened wing. Oliver, instantly perceiving the change of battle, galloped over the bridge of boats back to the troops he had left, passed over again his foot and horse, and fell upon the royal forces. These were quickly driven in, fighting desperately from point to point into the now closing shades of evening. Fort Royal, disdaining to yield to Cromwell's summons, was stormed, and all within it put to the sword. By eight o'clock the city gates were forced, and pell-mell the flying and the pursuers burst into the crowded streets. There a fearful carnage ensued. Fighting went on from street to street far into the night; and the city was delivered over to pillage. The overthrow was complete. Three thousand dead Scots lay on the field: 10,000 prisoners were taken. The remnant of the fugitives were cut down in the retreat; Hamilton, Derby, Massey, Lauderdale, Lesley, and all the leaders were taken prisoners. "My Lord-General did exceedingly hazard himself, riding up and down in the midst of the fire." It was "as stiff a contest for four or five hours as ever I have seen." The loss of the victors was under 200 men. "The dimensions of this mercy," wrote Cromwell to the Speaker, "are above my thoughts. It is, for aught I know, a crowning mercy." And then he breaks forth in the very hour of victory, as at Dunbar, as at Drogheda, as at Naseby, to impress on Parliament the great lessons which this mercy appeared to him to teach. Cromwell was right. The Royalist cause was utterly crushed out at Worcester. He never again appeared in the field; and during his lifetime the sword was not drawn again in England.

In many respects this last campaign differs much from all that went before it. In the month that elapsed, from 3rd August to the 3rd of September, the army that fought at Dunbar had marched 300 miles. New armies had been mustered in many counties, equipped, supplied, and made to converge by a common plan, had first controlled the Royalist invaders and then had hemmed them in, as in a circle of iron. Not a single scheme miscarried; and from the hour that Charles crossed the border he had never had a chance. And so too the battle of Worcester was far more complex than any which Cromwell had hitherto fought. The operations in which it culminated were carried on continuously for a whole week. The simultaneous attack on both sides of the city, and the advance along both sides of two rivers, was a very complex manoeuvre. To build two bridges of boats in mid-battle, to pass an army twice across a rapid river in the same engagement and within a few hours, is a bold and difficult achievement. It demanded in the troops an alertness and precision of discipline; in their officers experience and skill; and in their commander a consummate mastery of his resources and confidence in his men. It was fully justified by success. Not a single combination broke down. And this singular and complex battle would alone suffice to place the name of Cromwell high in the rank of tacticians, unless we judge his own impetuous courage to savour too much of the general of division.

Here Cromwell, at the age of fifty-two, sheathed the sword which he had girt on at the age of forty-three. To judge by the test of success, few generals have ever done more. Not only did he never command in any battle that did not result in utter ruin to his enemy, but no single operation of war that he ever undertook had failed. With some 15,000 men he practically reconquered Ireland in nine months; with a little larger force he subdued Scotland in about a year. At Marston and at Naseby he had converted a losing battle into an overwhelming victory. At Basing, at Drogheda, at Worcester, he stormed strong places, desperately defended, in a few hours of fighting and with very moderate loss. At Preston, with a loss of 50 men, he annihilated a brave army of 24,000 men; at Dunbar, with a smaller loss, he annihilated another brave army of 22,000; at Worcester, with a loss of under 200, he overwhelmed an army of 15,000 men. He never fared so well, he said, as when the enemy were two to one. Except at Worcester, he always fought against great odds. Every one of his victories was won in the least time and with the smallest loss. It is true that he was never opposed to an army at all equal in discipline to his own. But then the discipline, the *morale*, the organisation were all his work. He had created a regular army, and had trained it to become as perfect an instrument of war as history records. And thus, if we judge by results and the standard of his age, Oliver Cromwell stands out as thoroughly successful in strategy and as a general in the field such as our history records but one or two.

CHAPTER X

THE UNOFFICIAL DICTATORSHIP

A.D. 1651–1653. AETAT. 52–54

As the Second Civil War, leading up to the death of the king, had left Cromwell the foremost man in the nation in all but style and office, so he returned from the conquest of Ireland and Scotland, and the final overthrow of the royal cause at Worcester, invested with an undefined but semi-official dictatorship.

Parliament received the news of the victory with a spasm of relief and unbounded enthusiasm, and made the return of the Lord-General one long triumphal progress. A deputation from the House met him at Aylesbury; from Acton, the Speaker, the Lord Mayor, sheriffs, and a great assemblage of members and civic officials, conducted him in state to London with coaches, bodyguard, salvoes of artillery, and shouts of the crowd. He received the thanks of the House, an additional grant of £4000 a year, and the use of Hampton Court as a residence. Thereby he was recognised by what remained of legal authority as practically dictator.

He was now at the height of his power and prestige; and even Hugh Peters thought that he would make himself king. This, then, was the moment when a Bonaparte would have seized the vacant throne. Cromwell made no such use of the immense ascendancy which Drogheda, Dunbar, and Worcester had added to the office of Commander-in-Chief.

It was remarked that he carried himself with affability and modesty, and he betook himself to work as a simple member of the Council. There he laboured assiduously for nineteen months; nor on any single occasion did he bring himself conspicuously before the nation. His biographers have found it hard to ascertain how, during this period, his energies were employed. The history of his work is to be sought for in the records of the Council of State, and its manifold commissions and departments. He served on the standing committees of the Ordnance, of the Admiralty, of Trade and Foreign affairs, of Law, of the affairs of Ireland and Scotland, of the Dutch question, beside many other subsidiary committees for special matters. Of the army he was already the chief by Act of Parliament. Thus legally in control of the whole military forces, with paramount voice in the civil service, at once Captain-General and semi-official dictator, Oliver worked on at the administrative business of the nation. But he worked without display, accepting the shadowy authority of the remnant or fag-end of the Long Parliament. It was only after an anxious interval of abortive attempts at a settled government that he began to take independent action.

Nineteen months elapsed after Worcester fight before he closed the Long Parliament: it was two years and three months before he was named Protector.

The situation was that which inevitably succeeds a violent and successful revolution. The whole fabric of the body politic and social, had been shaken to its roots; the peril which had given the Commonwealth its cohesion and mighty force was at an end; and the various elements of which that force was composed were now free to insist on their differences. We may assume that the majority of the nation did not desire a permanent Commonwealth; that the Royalist party represented ideas and institutions to which Englishmen were destined to cling for generations, and even for centuries to come. On the other hand, the Commonwealth party, by their convictions, character, and organisation, by their superior weight of every sort, possessed an enormous predominance in effective strength.

The backbone of that Commonwealth party was the army—an army which consisted not of mercenaries or conscripts, but which was the flower of the people; men who were, and knew themselves to be, the natural leaders of their countrymen. They were at once an army made up of trained politicians, and a party made up of unconquered veterans. Rarely, indeed, in history has moral and material force been thus concentrated in a body, possessing both intense political conviction and consummate military discipline. They were the passion, the courage, the conscience of the people in arms; a political group, in energy and will stronger than all other groups together; a corps of soldiers who had no equals in Europe. They had none of the vices of an army; none of the restlessness of a political faction. Their political ideas were few, but very definite, and held with intense tenacity: religious freedom, orderly government, and the final abolition of the abuses for which Laud and Charles had died. In religion they were mainly Independents, seeking the widest liberty for themselves and others. Their wishes as soldiers were for peace, to return to their homes and to civil life. Devoted to their great chief, and profoundly trusting his honesty and wisdom, they maintained unbroken discipline within as well as without their body, leaving affairs of State to him and to his council of officers.

Parliament, or the thin residuum of the House of Commons which claimed that name, practically consisted of a junto of men who, after so many expulsions, purges, and abstentions of all sorts, continued to meet, to the average number of fifty, occasionally reaching a little more than one hundred. In spite of frequent siftings, the House was constantly gravitating back into the hands of lawyers and Presbyterians. The Council of State—of forty-one members, almost all members of Parliament—was only a committee of the House, where soldiers and administrators had predominant influence, and which virtually governed the nation. Cromwell, his officers, and a few men of action practically directed the Council. But it was far too large for an efficient cabinet; it was divided by very contrary views; and its activity was constantly impeded by the House which had appointed it.

It is fortunate that in our English revolution it is in no way necessary to disparage one set of men in order to do justice to their opponents. Both House and Council contained many men of great ability and character. Some of the stoutest and purest spirits in our history were in their number. There were indefatigable men of business, excellent administrators, keen and subtle brains, and above all, sterling honesty and excellent sense amongst them. In one or two there was a real vein of heroism and of sagacity. Still there was but one statesman of consummate genius; and that fact many of them were slow to recognise.

Cromwell, now inwardly assured that he had been called by God and by all good men to take the foremost place, stood apart from all the various sections by reason of his far wider grasp of the whole situation and his constructive and organising instinct. In his official despatch after the victory at Dunbar (4th September 1650) he had broken out to the Speaker with the abrupt appeal: "Believe the oppressed, hear the groans of poor prisoners in England. Be pleased to reform the abuses of all professions:—and if there be any one such that makes many poor to make a few rich, that suits not a Commonwealth." So now on the morrow of Worcester (4th September 1651) he again implored the House that "justice and righteousness, mercy and truth, may flow from you, as a thankful return to our gracious God."

Always strongly conservative, he set his face steadily towards "a settlement of this nation." Always zealous for social order, he looked directly for the mending of practical wrongs. The state of the Church, the state of the law, the manifold grievances and sufferings of men on all sides, and the confusion of all institutions and authorities, filled him with horror and pity. Everything in Church and State was alike provisional and chaotic. The scanty oligarchy which clung to the bare name of Parliament—a Parliament which had been summoned by King Charles eleven years ago—never could be accepted by the nation as its genuine representative in the great change of government. The Episcopal Church was suppressed, yet the Presbyterian Church was not set up on any permanent or complete basis. The House continually and fitfully interfered in religious questions, from the point of view of rigid Presbyterian orthodoxy. The Royalists were still harried with the most crushing exactions, and held everything on sufferance. The relations with foreign countries were precarious, and with the Dutch they were hostile.

The law in especial manner was in a state of chaos. There were 23,000 unheard cases waiting in Chancery; and this was a perpetual grievance both to the general and his soldiers. It might surprise us to find the army and its chief so constantly troubled about the abuses of the law, did we not remember that the Civil War was the turning-point in the history of English law; that it shattered the whole system of feudal tenure, and with the Restoration we find the land law mainly what it continued to be down to the present century. The period of transition was a time of chaos and injustice, and Cromwell and his Ironsides were men to whom social injustice and official tyranny never appealed in vain. But, besides the law, practical questions had to be solved. An army of 50,000 men had to be reduced to one-half. A mass of diseased and wretched prisoners had to be disposed of; the fortresses and castles dismantled, reduced, or repaired. Ireland and Scotland had to be brought into permanent settlement. In one word, a nation which had been torn by ten years of desperate civil war, and of which every institution had been passing through a crisis, lay waiting for order, settlement, and reorganisation.

The difficulties were all grouped round two great questions: "the settlement of the nation" and a "new representative "; or, as we should now say, a permanent constitution and a new Parliament. Without the former, Cromwell saw, everything remained an open question; no man could feel secure, and peace would never begin. Without the latter, no reform was possible in Church, law, taxation, or in legal or civil reorganisation. The Council of State and its commissions sufficed for daily administration. The army, the navy, the ordnance, Ireland and Scotland, and the treasury, were managed with energy and skill. But in order to settle ecclesiastical and legal questions, to close the system of confiscation, and to return to regular government, legislation was necessary. And for practical legislation the House was incompetent. The lawyers, the Presbyterians, the reactionists, and the pedants debated each Bill for months. The House drifted into a permanent attitude of reaction; by turns learned, loquacious, impracticable, self-important, and bigoted.

Cromwell was bent on a "settlement," the difficulties of which he clearly saw. He showed such a willingness to come to terms with the defeated party, and such real sympathy with their protracted sufferings, that the sterner spirits at once accused him of gaining the goodwill of the loyalists to serve his own designs. He plainly saw that the nation was not prepared for a definite republic; nor had he himself any preference for it. He also saw, as the lawyers continually showed him, that without some monarchical element, the English constitution, the English scheme of government and of law, could scarcely be got into work again. For a reorganisation of the body politic, as distinct from its complete transformation, a person as ruler was essential. Cromwell was profoundly convinced of this; and as a matter of law and of history he was plainly right. The difficulties were, however, not slight. The army and the zealous Puritans were against the very name of king, and especially averse to any prince of the late king's house. The lawyers, on the other hand, could not conceive of the monarchical element in any other form. Cromwell's own mind inclined towards a personal head of the State, though he still shrunk from the name of king.

Nothing can be plainer than this, that his whole soul rejected the idea of a mere Parliamentary executive: government vested in a single elective chamber. By character, from experience, and by conviction, he was rooted to the idea of a double authority: a person permanently charged with the executive, and a coordinate elected legislature. The whole future history of England lay in this struggle—the alternative of the American system with its distinct personal executive, or the modern British system of a single supreme Parliament having the executive as a part and creature of itself. After many fluctuations and an irregular epoch of oligarchy, the Parliamentary system of government triumphed; and for a century at least it has kept undisputed ascendancy. But it is not proved thereby that Cromwell was wrong.

The struggle between Cromwell and the House was on neither side a question of personal ambition. It was a struggle between two far-reaching principles of government; the struggle as to whether executive authority shall be subordinate to, or co-ordinate with, the legislature. It was at bottom the same principle which, under very various forms and with very different aims, great English statesmen have more or less asserted—Elizabeth, Strafford, Cromwell, William III., Walpole, and Chatham; and which the founders of the American constitution successfully worked out across the Atlantic. Parliamentary executive is still the great problem of our time. After Worcester it presented itself for the first time in our history; claiming to be a permanent and dominant institution. Within a few days of Cromwell's return, the question of the new Parliament was raised, evidently at his desire. For three months the question was revived and pressed, until, at last, after repeated divisions and debates, the House was induced, by a majority of two, to vote its dissolution. This it fixed for a date three years distant, 3rd November 1654. But in the meantime many things were to happen.

Around the great question at issue between Cromwell and the House, the minor questions were grouped. Cromwell and the army clung to entire freedom of worship; the House to Presbyterian orthodoxy. Cromwell now felt himself to be in the higher sense the representative of the nation, the guardian of the interests of all, even of those he had defeated. The Parliament men, filled with pride in their successful revolution, could not see that the time had come for putting an end to revolution. Cromwell insisted on an amnesty and on closing the system of confiscation; the House would not resign the revolutionary expedient of raising supplies. Cromwell's strength rested on the army; the House sought to reduce it in order to strengthen the navy. Mainly for political objects, Vane and his party plunged into the Dutch war. Cromwell and his soldiers were for making a short cut to practical reforms; the House, with its lawyers and officials, saw obstacles and dangers in every reform. As the army trusted its cause to Cromwell, so the House was represented by Vane, its most eminent leader, a man as heroic and generous as Cromwell himself, of varied capacity and unwearied energy. Both Cromwell and Vane represented parties who had borne the heat and burden of the day, and who had done great things for the common cause, the one in the field, the other in council. Neither party could claim the majority of the nation; perhaps both together could not claim it. Parliament, now alike unpopular and incompetent, had nothing but a shred of legal right. But Cromwell wielded overwhelming force, and embodied the hopes and the trust of the best men.

Immediately on his return from Worcester, Cromwell found himself addressed by petitions for the redress of grievances, in the matter of law, of imprisonment, of exactions, of tithes, as to one, said the petitioners, into whose hands the sword was put. And commissions were actually issued to officers to hear and determine civil cases, which gave great satisfaction to the parties. The Lord-General was thus passing by consent into the position of general Moderator. It was at this time that Whitelocke places the famous discussion he records as to the settlement of the nation. Cromwell, he says, desired a meeting between the leaders in Parliament and the chiefs of the army. There he very plainly stated the issue thus: whether a republic or a mixed monarchical government will be best; and if anything monarchical, then in whom that power should be placed? The lawyers were for a mixed monarchy; the generals for a republic. "The laws of England are so interwoven with the power and practice of a monarchy," said Whitelocke, "that to settle a government without something of monarchy in it" would lead to incalculable inconveniences. He and others evidently inclined to a restoration of one of the Stuart princes. The generals asked why not a republic as well as other nations? Cromwell, it is clear, objected to any recall of the princes; but he thought "that a settlement of somewhat with monarchical power in it would be very effectual." It is plain that from this time he gave it to be understood that he desired a settlement with himself invested with some monarchical power; though, as to the name or prerogative of king, he felt and continued to feel the deepest hesitation and doubt.

The question was indeed one of extraordinary complication and difficulty. Legally speaking, the whole fabric of the body politic, the daily routine of law and of administration, centred in the name and authority of the king. A king *de facto*, with or without hereditary right, even a usurper, fulfilled the legal conditions. By a statute of Henry VII. acts done under the authority of a *de facto* king, even a usurper, were not acts of treason. But without a *de facto* king, the old system of law and order would have to be remodelled from its base. Between the Puritan chiefs and the royal house an indelible bar seemed set. One might be a lawful king, who had conquered his throne by the sword or had been called in by Parliament; but a king without trace of royal blood was undreamed of in England. The gulf that separated the most absolute military ruler, from the same man regularly proclaimed king was immense— legally, morally, and socially. But then what would bring soldiers like Harrison, politicians like Vane, to acquiesce in the proclamation of *Oliver Rex*? The problem was perhaps insoluble. In the meantime Cromwell worked towards a settlement to have in it somewhat of a monarchical power, and left the issue to time.

All through the year 1652 the struggle went on, Cromwell and his officers continually pressing the House to complete the reforms and settle a new Parliament; the House eternally debating, obstinately bent on retaining its legal autocracy. The story of the contest was told by Oliver most truthfully and simply in his public speeches. He and his soldiers were resolved, he said, that the nation should reap the fruit of all the blood and treasure that had been spent in the cause. The officers had begun by private appeals to the House: in August they presented a petition embodying their demands—provision for preaching the Gospel, removal of scandalous ministers, reform of the law, redress of abuses in excise, in tithes, in the treasury, and lastly, provision for a new Parliament. They got no answer but a few words. Then, "finding the People dissatisfied in every corner of the nation, and laying at our doors the non-performance of these things," Cromwell declares that he called a series of meetings between the leaders in Parliament and the chiefs of the army. Ten or twelve such meetings were held without result.

In November Cromwell met Whitelocke, and asked him "to consider the dangerous condition we are all in." The members of Parliament, he said, were become odious to the army for their pride and ambition and self-seeking, their delays of business and their design to perpetuate themselves to continue the power in their hands, for their meddling in private matters, for their injustice and partiality, and the scandalous lives of some of the chief of them. People open their mouths against them, he said; and they cannot be kept within bounds of justice and law or reason, for there is none superior or coordinate with them. "What," said he abruptly, "if a man should take upon him to be king?" Whitelocke implored him to consider the danger and the evil, and urged a compromise with Charles Stuart. "That," said Cromwell, "is a matter of so high importance and difficulty, that it deserves more of consideration and debate."

The House, led by Vane, now altered its tactics, and began to press on a Bill for a new representation, a plan which, with much parade of free election, was simply a scheme to perpetuate themselves. The existing members were to sit without re-election, and were to form an exclusive tribunal for admitting new members. It was a transparent artifice to continue themselves, whilst adding such additional members as they might approve. Cromwell thereupon called another conference at his own house. Some twenty-three members attended on the 19th April 1653. There he and the generals told the Parliament men clearly that they would not suffer them to pass such an Act. They proposed as an alternative a temporary commission of forty leading men to summon a new Parliament. The sitting ended late at night without decision; it was agreed to meet the next day, with an understanding that in the meantime the Act should not be passed.

The next day the conference was renewed at Cromwell's lodgings. There news was brought that the House was hastily passing the obnoxious measure. Presently Colonel Ingoldsby came in from the House to tell the general that not a moment was to be lost, if he meant to do anything. Furious at what he believed, perhaps without reason, to be the bad faith of Vane and the leaders, he called a company of musketeers to attend him, and with Lambert and other officers, strode silently to the House. In plain black clothes and gray worsted stockings, the Lord-General came in quietly and took his seat, as Vane was pressing the House to pass the dissolution Bill without delay and without the customary forms. He beckoned to Harrison and told him that the Parliament was ripe for dissolution, and he must do it. "Sir," said Harrison, "the work is very great and dangerous."—"You say well," said the general, and thereupon sat still for about a quarter of an hour. Vane sat down, and the Speaker was putting the question for passing the Bill. Then said Cromwell to Harrison again, "This is the time; I must do it." He rose up, put off his hat, and spoke.

Beginning moderately and respectfully, he presently changed his style, told them of their injustice, delays of justice, self-interest, and other faults; charging them not to have a heart to do anything for the public good, to have espoused the corrupt interest of Presbytery and the lawyers, who were the supporters of tyranny and oppression, accusing them of an intention to perpetuate themselves in power. And rising into passion, "as if he were distracted," he told them that the Lord had done with them, and had chosen other instruments for the carrying on His work that were worthy. Sir Peter Wentworth rose to complain of such language in Parliament, coming from their own trusted servant. Roused to fury by the interruption, Cromwell left his seat, clapped on his hat, walked up and down the floor of the House, stamping with his feet, and cried out, "You are no Parliament, I say you are no Parliament. Come, come, we have had enough of this; I will put an end to your prating. Call them in!" Twenty or thirty musketeers under Colonel Worsley marched in on to the floor of the House. The rest of the guard were placed at the door and in the lobby.

Vane from his place cried out, "This is not honest, yea, it is against morality and common honesty." Cromwell, who evidently regarded Vane as the breaker of the supposed agreement, turned on him with a loud voice, crying, "O Sir Henry Vane, Sir Henry Vane, the Lord deliver me from Sir Henry Vane." Then looking upon one of the members, he said, "There sits a drunkard;" to another he said, "Some of you are unjust, corrupt persons, and scandalous to the profession of the Gospel." "Some are whoremasters," he said, looking at Wentworth and Marten. Going up to the table, he said, "What shall we do with this Bauble? Here take it away!" and gave it to a musketeer. "Fetch him down," he cried to Harrison, pointing to the Speaker. Lenthall sat still, and refused to come down unless by force. "Sir," said Harrison, "I will lend you my hand," and putting his hand within his, the Speaker came down. Algernon Sidney sat still in his place. "Put him out," said Cromwell. And Harrison and Worsley put their hands on his shoulders, and he rose and went out. The members went out, fifty-three in all, Cromwell still calling aloud. To Vane he said that he might have prevented this; but that he was a juggler and had not common honesty. "It is you," he said, as they passed him, "that have forced me to do this, for I have sought the Lord night and day, that He would rather slay me than put me on the doing of this work." He snatched the Bill of dissolution from the hand of the clerk, put it under his cloak, seized on the records, ordered the guard to clear the House of all members, and to have the door locked, and went away to Whitehall.

Such is one of the most famous scenes in our history, that which of all other things has most heavily weighed on the fame of Cromwell. In truth it is a matter of no small complexity, which neither constitutional eloquence nor boisterous sarcasm has quite adequately unravelled. Both in essence and in form much may be said on both sides. Perhaps even more than the act in itself, the mode and the circumstances have caused indignation and offence. It is one of the rare occasions in all history where a great act of State has been carried out with personal fury and outrage. And it is hard to imagine the end which personal fury and outrage can serve. There was no other public occasion on which Cromwell displayed ungovernable passion. But he was a man of volcanic temper, at all times liable to outbursts of coarseness. From his youth he was given to moody frenzies and ecstatic outpourings of the inmost soul.

The practice of Bible expounding in the camp had developed in him an unctuous and heated mannerism. At times in battle, we have seen, he seemed deliberately to fling off all control, as when at Drogheda and at Worcester he dashed into the fray with a fury which can hardly be forgiven in a supreme commander. The story reads to us as if Cromwell, resolved not to be checkmated by the Bill, had not quite decided how in detail he would act. Then committing himself to an unbridled rage, in the consciousness of overpowering force and a direct mission from God, he let the whole torrent of his will and of his scorn boil over in the sight of all men.

In strict constitutional right the House was no more the Parliament than Cromwell was the king. A House of Commons, which had executed the king, abolished the Lords, approved the *coup d'état* of Pride, and by successive proscriptions had reduced itself to a few score of extreme partisans, had no legal title to the name of Parliament. The junto which held to Vane was not more numerous than the junto which held to Cromwell; they had far less public support; nor had their services to the Cause been so great. In closing the House, the Lord-General had used his office of Commander-in-Chief to anticipate one *coup d'état* by another. Had he been ten minutes late, Vane would himself have dissolved the House; snapping a vote which would give his faction a legal ascendancy. Yet, after all, the fact remains that Vane and the remnant of the famous Long Parliament had that *scintilla juris*, as lawyers call it, that semblance of legal right which counts for so much in things political. Civil society is held together by conventional respect for legalised authority. And in the shipwreck of the Constitution some *tabula in naufragio*, to use a legal metaphor, still rested in the hands of the few score members who remained. History and Englishmen have not yet forgiven the great soldier who broke through this ancient conventional respect, tearing down a legal *simulacrum*, useless and obstructive as it long had been. In the mind of Cromwell, always impatient of legal conventions, the urgent call of public duty and the manifest favour of Heaven outweighed all the evils which must have been suggested to him by his prudence, his sagacity, and his wonderful knowledge of men.

His deed must be judged by its results and its essence. Was it good, was it necessary, for Cromwell to anticipate Vane? Were the moral forces with Vane or with Cromwell? The technical rights of either were shadowy enough; the act took place in mid-revolution and utter chaos; public confidence was in no way shaken. So stated, it is plain that it was Cromwell, and not Vane, who could give the nation peace, good government, legal, social, and religious reform. It was Cromwell, and not Vane, who had behind him the effective weight of the nation. If Cromwell had in numbers less than a majority of the people, Vane had behind him nothing but an unpopular and divided faction. Coarse and violent as was Cromwell's conduct, high-minded and patriotic as was Vane's nature, Cromwell was a mighty statesman, and Vane was only a noble character. The final judgment of history must come back to the prevalent opinion of the time: that, outside a small group of partisans and doctrinaire republicans, no man regretted Cromwell's act. A year and a half later he said in Parliament:

> "I told them,—for I knew it better than any one man in the Parliament could know it; because of my manner of life which was to run up and down the nation, thereby giving me to see and know the temper and spirits of all men, and of the best of men,—that the Nation loathed their sitting, I knew it. And, so far as I could discern, when they were

> dissolved, there was not so much as the barking of a dog, or any general or visible repining at it! You are not a few here present who can assert this as well as myself."

Returning to Whitehall, Cromwell found the officers still in council, and after some expressions of dissent, he satisfied them of the justice of his act. In the afternoon, attended by Lambert and Harrison, he went down to the Council of State. He told them that there was no place for them there, as the Parliament was dissolved. Bradshaw, Scott, Haslerig, and others protested, and then, without more words, withdrew. Three days later a long, elaborate, and Biblical document appeared, as the "Declaration of the Lord-General and his Council of Officers." It evidently embodies Cromwell's own mind, if it were not written by his hand, and entirely agrees with the account given in his speeches. It asserted that the honest people of the nation and the army, having sought the Lord, felt it to be a duty to secure the cause and to establish righteousness and peace in these nations; as the late Parliament were seeking to perpetuate themselves, they had been necessitated to put an end to it. It concluded with a long sermon on the duty of godly men; and order was given that all judges, sheriffs, mayors, and other civil officers should proceed in the execution of their respective offices. Within a few days came in declarations of adhesion from the navy, the armies in Scotland and in Ireland, and addresses from municipal and civic bodies. There were no resignations, no arrests, no further force. The fighting men approved, the officials obeyed, the nation acquiesced. And without a show of opposition, the whole machinery of the State passed quietly into the strong hand of Cromwell.

He was determined that it should be no military despotism. Resolute as he was that there should be a person as head of the State, he was equally resolute that the government should be a civil government, with an elected legislature, a Parliament to vote taxes and make laws, and an executive bound in legal limits. What he did, he told the Little Parliament, was not to grasp at the power himself, or to keep it in military hands, no, not for a day; but to put it into the hands of proper persons that might be called from the several parts of the nation. Ten days after the close of the Long Parliament Cromwell issued a further declaration in his own name, that Parliament being dissolved, persons of approved fidelity and honesty were to be called from the several parts of this Commonwealth to the supreme authority, and in the meantime a Council of State should be constituted. An interim Council of thirteen, four of them civilians, was appointed; and summonses were issued to diverse persons to undertake the "Trust" of the government of the Commonwealth. In the meantime for nine weeks Oliver continued to govern, by the advice of the Council and his officers.

Some hundred and forty summonses were issued by Cromwell to "persons fearing God, and of approved fidelity and honesty"—names mainly suggested, it seems, by the "godly clergy." Some were men of rank and fortune; eighteen had sat in the Long Parliament; Monk and Blake and some soldiers were members, and some were extreme types of the Puritan sects. Only two did not attend. They met on the 4th of July 1653; they sat five months; passed some useful measures, raised many burning questions, were named the Little Parliament. Cromwell opened the sitting with a long and powerful speech. He began by the story of the civil wars; how God had raised up a poor and contemptible company of men and given them success, simply by their owning a principle of godliness and religion. How the Long Parliament had become impracticable; how in many months together they had failed to settle one word, "incumbrances"; how, as they had neglected all their duties, they had been dissolved. How the general, anxious "to divest the sword of all power in the civil administration, had summoned them that he might devolve the burden on their shoulders." In thus calling them to the exercises of the supreme authority, he that means to be their servant takes occasion to offer them some charge. Then he bursts into an impassioned sermon, taking texts from the prophets, the psalms, the epistles—a sermon rich with grand passages, with quaint, homely, vivid phrases, such as Bunyan might have uttered, fatherly exhortations to righteousness and trust in God. Finally he turns again to his favourite psalm, the 68th, the psalm he sang on the field of Dunbar: "Let God arise, let his enemies be scattered: let them also that hate him flee before him. . . . The earth shook, the heavens also dropped in the presence of God. . . . The chariots of God are twenty thousand, even thousands of angels: the Lord is among them, as in Sinai, in the holy place." "And indeed," cries out the Puritan soldier, "the triumph of that psalm is exceeding high and great; and God is accomplishing it." Never before in the history of England was Parliament opened by speech like that.

This is the first of those speeches of Cromwell to his Parliament, some nineteen in all, which are amongst the most precious records of history. Now that laborious love has unveiled them to us, we can look down through them into the inmost spirit of the man. Uncouth, tangled, and periphrastic as much in them seems to us, wrapped up in a Biblical verbiage which has long been confined to the pulpit, ill-reported, full of broken sentences and confused periods, there is yet in them an innate majesty and truthfulness; nay, eloquence; even poetry and pathos. We hear the very beat of a great, generous heart; we see the flash of an heroic temper, full of trust, of sublime desires, of unshaken courage. The religious hopes are not ours; the cast of mind is one which only by an effort can we picture to ourselves; the mixture of practical business with the promises and manifestations of God to the saints is to us so strange as to sound hardly sane. Yet such is the greatest attempt ever made in history to found a civil society on the literal words of Scripture. So deep is the gulf which, in things spiritual, two centuries and a half have set between them and us.

The doings of this assembly of Puritan notables need not detain us. Cromwell plainly designed them to be a constituent, not a permanent body; to call a regular Parliament; and to exercise provisional authority. There never was before, he said, a supreme authority so called, 140 persons not one but had in him faith in Jesus Christ. He plainly told them that they had the affairs of the nation committed to them; that the existing Council of State held power only in the interim; that it rested with them to continue this Council or appoint another. In his third speech (12th September 1654) he called God to witness that his chief end in summoning them was to divest himself of the absolute power in his hands, as he desired not to live for a day in the unlimited condition of boundless authority. But as he afterwards amply confessed, this assembly of godly persons was an utter failure. They did good and vigorous work. They sought to abolish the Court of Chancery; they undertook to frame a code of law; they proceeded to reform the Church, to abolish tithes, Church patronage, and to establish civil marriage. All this done in the trenchant spirit of religious fervour, which alarmed all interests, and aroused every class. The Church, property, law, society seemed threatened by reformers who were prepared, Bible in hand, to dispose at once of every question of the day. Cromwell, intensely conservative by habit, and a keen observer of public opinion, grew uneasy when he saw the reign of the saints beginning in earnest. Four years later he publicly confessed his own folly and weakness, admitting that these godly men were going straight to "confusion of all things": would have "swallowed up all civil and religious interest, and brought us under the horridest arbitrariness that ever was exercised in the world." In him godliness never for a moment overpowered his instinct for the practical and the politic. In them godliness was enough, and all things and all men were unworthy to be set in the scale. The indignation without rose to fury. Such root-and-branch reformation of all institutions on a pure Biblical basis was being attempted by men who had no constituents, no real power, who were mostly unknown nominees of a religious party. By a politic *coup-de-main*, the majority, perceiving the situation, suddenly resigned their powers to the general who had given them.

Parliament and Council of State departed, Cromwell was left as the sole legalised authority in the nation. But he had no intention of holding authority alone. He summoned his Council of officers and other persons of interest. Within a few days it was announced that the Council had offered, and he had accepted the style of Lord Protector of the Commonwealth, to carry on the government by the advice of a Council and with an Instrument of Government, or written Constitution. By this charter the government was vested in a Protector, a Council of thirteen at least and twenty-one at most, and the Commons of England, Scotland, and Ireland, meeting in triennial Parliament, the first to begin on 3rd September 1654. All Bills that they passed were to become law, even without the Protector's assent, after twenty days. Until the sitting of Parliament, the Protector and his Council had power to make Ordinances, having the force of law. The office of Protector was to be elective, to be chosen by the Council.

On 16th of December 1653 Oliver was formally installed with some simple state. He became a constitutional and strictly limited sovereign for life.

CHAPTER XI

THE PROTECTORATE

A.D. 1653–1658. AETAT. 54–59

From his installation, on 16th December 1653, until his death, 3rd September 1658, a period of nearly five years, Oliver held supreme power as Protector of the Commonwealth. His task now was to control the Revolution which he had led to victory; and his career enters on a new and yet greater phase. He stands out amongst the very few men in all history who, having overthrown an ancient system of government, have proved themselves with even greater success to be constructive and conservative statesmen. In this giant's task Oliver had the sympathy and devotion of many of the truest lovers of liberty, justice, and religion. But he had against him Vane, Hutchinson, Ludlow, Bradshaw, Sidney, Haslerig, and many a noble friend of his manhood, to whom the Revolution meant republican equality even more than liberty, and legal right even more than order and prosperity. He had against him too another group of earnest Commonwealth men, to whom the struggle meant a religious and social revolution—men like the austere enthusiast Harrison, the frantic Sexby, and the zealot Overton, the friend of Milton. Of the men who had made the Revolution, some were doctrinaire republicans, some were Bible fanatics, some were constitutional martinets, some were socialist dreamers. Oliver was no one of these;

and such men were all from the first his opponents. But he had with him the Puritan rank and file, the great majority of the superior officers, such clear and lofty spirits as those of Milton and Marvell, Blake and Lockhart, Lawrence and Lisle; the men of business; all moderate men of every party who desired peace, order, good government; the great cities; the army and the navy. With these, and his own commanding genius, he held his own triumphantly, slowly winning the confidence of the nation by virtue of unbroken success and (as it seemed) miraculous fortune. Thus he grew ever larger, until he lay in his last sleep murmuring, "My work is done:" in battle, a soldier who had never met with a reverse, so a statesman who in a supreme place had never met with a fall.

Cromwell was, and felt himself to be, a dictator called in by the winning cause in a revolution to restore confidence and secure peace. He was, as he said frequently, "the Constable set to keep order in the Parish." Nor was he in any sense a military despot. He was no professional soldier; and he had no taste for arbitrary or martial rule. He was a citizen and a country gentleman, who at the age of forty-three first girt on his sword in earnest, and at the age of fifty-two had put it off. Though he distrusted and disliked a Parliamentary executive, he clung to a civil and legal executive. From first to last after the closing of the Long Parliament, he struggled for five years to realise his fixed idea of a dual government—neither a Dictator without a Parliament, nor a Parliament without a Head of the Executive. With dogged iteration he repeats—the government shall rest with a Single Person and a Parliament, the Parliament making all laws and voting all supplies, co-ordinate with the authority of the Chief Person, and not meddling with the executive. This was his idea—an idea which the people of England have rejected, but which the people of America have adopted. More than a century later the founders of the United States revived and established Oliver's ideal, basing it upon popular election, a thing which, in 1654, was impossible in England.

Never did a ruler invested with absolute power and overwhelming military force more obstinately strive to surround his authority with legal limits and Parliamentary control. The possession of boundless power and arbitrary authority, even as a temporary expedient, seemed to have in it something which alarmed and shocked his nature. Absolute as he was after his triumphal return from Worcester, he deliberately sank his personality for nineteen months in the routine of his office, and laboured indirectly to get the work done by Parliament. Ten days after closing the Long Parliament he announced the summoning of a Convention Parliament. When that suddenly dissolved itself, within a few days he procured the Instrument of Government to be drawn, without which he refused the office of Protector. This Instrument involved the election of a new Parliament, on the footing of the admirable Reform Bill sketched out by Ireton and completed by Vane. By it the Protector was placed in the position of a strictly limited king, on the lines of the constitution, but with new Parliamentary prerogatives. Not only was the Protector bound by Parliament, but he was bound by the Council, which was not removable by him. The Instrument of Government was a constitution of a strictly limited type. And it was the basis of Oliver's authority as Protector.

During the five years of his supreme power, from the end of the Long Parliament, Oliver summoned three Parliaments, and the longest period in which he ruled without one was a year and eight months. Parliaments he did not like; did not understand; and managed with indifferent skill. He preferred a council, or a committee, for business. But he never repudiated the principle that laws and taxes are the necessary function of Parliament alone. The free election of Parliament on a really democratic basis he saw was impossible, at the risk of ruining the cause and re-opening the Civil War. Therein he was plainly right; and as a matter of constitutional law, all that can be said is, that in mid-revolution normal institutions are not always workable. What he thought practicable and safe with the only materials at hand, that he patiently endeavoured to effect. Most certain it is that he was no Parliamentary leader, and never could become one. His genius and nature had none of the elements which go to the making of a born chief of a Parliament. His intolerance of conventions, his scorn of eloquent egoism, his abhorrence of obstruction, delay, and waste, his intense masterfulness and passion for action, made him unfit for Parliamentary work. Both morally and intellectually he was not made to play the part of a Walpole or a Pitt. From the first his Protectorate was hampered by the fact that, though he recognised a Parliament as indispensable, he was by nature and training unendowed with Parliamentary tact. The forces of our race were against him. For the fortunes of England have for more than a century required Parliamentary skill as the secret of success in a statesman. And it has been our misfortune too seldom to recognise the genius of a ruler, where there is conspicuously absent the genius of the debater.

The question at issue was one of surpassing interest, which constitutional lawyers have never fully seized. As the English Commonwealth was the first example in modern Europe of a people sitting in judgment on their king and converting a kingdom into a republic, so the Instrument of Government was the first example of a long line of written constitutions. The fixed idea of Cromwell was the fixed idea of the founders of the United States of America, and of nearly every known continental system. There should be, he thought, a written Instrument; there should be an Executive Authority, not directly subordinate to Parliament; and there should be what Oliver called "fundamentals," or what we now call "constitutional guarantees"—fundamental bases not alterable like ordinary laws. England is the one country in the modern world where "fundamentals" or "constitutional guarantees" are unknown. And on the opening of a new republican era in England Cromwell's position was exactly that of Washington, of Hamilton, Jay, and Madison. The fixed idea of Vane, Bradshaw, Haslerig, and all the greater Parliamentarians, was to establish the autocracy of an elected House, supreme over the Executive, and free from any constitutional limit, just as we see it to-day. It was a momentous issue, nobly represented on both sides. That there was no Supreme Court, no constitutional arbiter, no appeal to the nation, was inevitable in the situation. The ideal of Vane and his friends was not established conclusively until the time of Pitt—130 years later, and the event proved how right Oliver was in insisting that in mid-revolution, with half the nation indifferent or hostile, it meant simple chaos.

From this point Oliver's life is the history of England, a history which could not be told in detail within the limits of this book. It will be best to concentrate his five years of power under three heads, which will form as many chapters; so as to devote the first to the general political position of the Protector, the second to his home administration, the last to his foreign policy. In his great task, Oliver had to aid him soldiers, seamen, diplomatists, and administrators, as able as any that ever served a king; but we miss nearly all the great names of the Civil Wars. The grand, pure figure of Ireton, the true founder of the Commonwealth, the one hero of the war who came nearest to Oliver, is gone. He died of fever in Ireland (November 1651). Ludlow, the contriver of Pride's Purge, the stalwart republican, honest heart and fine soldier, is soon to withdraw in disgust. Harrison, the noble fanatic, the right hand of Oliver when he closed the Long Parliament, the leader in the Parliament of Saints, was to pass much of the Protectorate in prison. As he said in his proud defiance to his judges, "When I found those that were as the apple of mine eye to turn aside, I did loathe them, and suffered imprisonment many years." Lambert, the second soldier of the Civil Wars, the real author of the

Protectorate, was still loyal to Oliver. Blake, Monk, Fleetwood, Lockhart, Broghill, Skippon, Wolseley, commanded his forces. In his Council and offices were some of the ablest men who have ever served this country. But the glory of his rule is John Milton. By a rare or unexampled fortune, the first political genius of his age was served by the greatest literary genius of his time. Cromwell and Milton stand forth as inseparable types: the Puritan statesman, the Puritan poet. Milton, who was appointed Foreign Secretary to the Council almost upon the establishment of the Commonwealth, served throughout the Protectorate of Oliver. It was during Oliver's struggle with the Long Parliament (1652) that he wrote his famous sonnet, "Cromwell, our chief of Men." It was upon the establishment of the Protectorate (May 1654) that he published the magnificent panegyric in the *Defensio Secunda*:

> "We are deserted, Cromwell; you alone remain; the sum-total of our affairs has come back to you, and hangs on you alone; we all yield to your insuperable worth. ... In human society there is nothing more pleasing to God, more agreeable to reason, nothing fairer and more useful to the State, than that the worthiest should bear rule."

Never had ruler so mighty a poet in his service; never did poet share such labours of State under so great a chief.

Oliver had learned a severe lesson from the failure of the godly persons in the Little Parliament. Till then he had cherished the belief that, though Parliament had failed, though Presbyterians were tyrannical, lawyers self-seeking, the rich profligate, and the mass of men worldly, yet the cause would triumph if the godly could be placed in absolute power for a time. He had placed them in power; and he had seen the Commonwealth tending to "confusion in all things." From that hour Oliver recovered his common sense. He saw that even the godly were prone to tyranny, folly, and mischief; and he saw the still greater difficulty of ascertaining who the godly are. Here, as always, Oliver proved to be a thorough conservative. As he opposed all democratic ideas of unrestricted appeal to the suffrage; as he had crushed the Levellers when they assailed property; so he shrank from the social revolution dreamed of by the Bible saints. He told his first Parliament: "As to the authority in the Nation; to the Magistracy; to the Banks and Orders of men—whereby England hath been known for hundreds of years—a nobleman, a gentleman, a yeoman; that is a good interest of the Nation and a great one!" Never again did he risk a real Reign of the Saints. He grew in his notions of statecraft ever wider, more practical, more tolerant. He relied more firmly on his carnal judgment; he came to see the strong sides of many persuasions. Like all great men, by the exercise of responsible power, Oliver grew and broadened continually.

By the Instrument of Government Parliament was to meet on 3rd of September; and in the nine months that intervened Oliver was to govern by means of Ordinances. He issued in that period some eighty-two, of various purport and of great importance. The Church, the Preachers, Chancery, the Treasury, Ireland, Scotland, Police, Public Order, Education, Taxation, are all dealt with in the form of Acts of Parliament. A most advantageous peace was made with the Dutch. And treaties of alliance or commerce were concluded with Sweden, with Denmark, and with Portugal. France and Spain were bidding against each other for the alliance of England. On the very day when Count Sa, the Portuguese minister, signed the treaty, Cromwell beheaded Don Pantaleon Sa, his brother, who had been dragged from the embassy, tried and convicted of murder. The Protector's government was at once seen to be the most powerful in Europe. He now removed to Whitehall, assumed the State of a supreme ruler, signed *Oliver P.*, and was king in all but name.

Oliver addressed his first Protectorate Parliament on Sunday, the 3rd of September:

> "Gentlemen," he said, "you are met here on the greatest occasion that, I believe, England ever saw; having upon your shoulders the Interests of three great Nations with the territories belonging to them; and truly, I believe I may say it without any hyperbole, you have upon your shoulders the interest of all the Christian people in the world." He expatiated on the confusion in the State, and told them the great end before them was Healing and Settling. The ten years' civil war had led the country to the brink of social dissolution, and to spiritual chaos. Liberty of conscience and liberty of the subject were being abused for the patronising of villanies. The Fifth Monarchy men would impose again the Judaical Law. Nothing was in the hearts and minds of men but "Overturn, overturn, overturn!" whilst the common Enemy sleeps not. Abroad the dangers were abating, but were still great. There was Scotland; there was Ireland to settle:—great tasks on all sides. And the Protector implored them, "not as one having dominion over them, but as their fellow-servant," to apply themselves to the great works upon their hands.

It was not to be. Immediately, under the leadership of old Parliamentarians, Haslerig, Scott, Bradshaw, and many other republicans, the House proceeded to debate the Instrument of Government, the constitutional basis of the existing system. By five votes, it decided to discuss "whether the House should approve of government by a Single Person and a Parliament." This was of course to set up the principle of making the Executive dependent on the House; a principle, in Oliver's mind, fatal to settlement and order. He acted at once. Calling on the Lord Mayor to secure the city, and disposing his own guard round Westminster Hall, he summoned the House again on the ninth day, and again addressed to them an earnest and powerful appeal.

> They were, he said, a free Parliament, provided they recognised the authority which had called them together. "I called not myself to this place! God and the People of these nations have borne testimony to it. God and the People

shall take it from me, else I will not part with it. I should be false to the trust that God hath placed in me, and to the interest of the People of these nations, if I did." Then he tells the story of his own calling; that he hoped to have leave to retire into private life; that the Long Parliament was becoming an intolerable tyranny when he closed it; that the Little Parliament of Saints was a failure; that on their resignation, he was left the only authority, a person having power over three Nations, without bound or limit set:—not very ill beloved by the Armies nor by the People. The Nation was in such a state that all Government was dissolved, and nothing left to keep things in order but the Sword. They who held the Sword had called him to be Protector. His nomination had been accepted by the City of London, many cities, boroughs, and counties; the judges, justices, sheriffs, and other officials had acted under his authority. Lastly, the Parliament itself met there under his writs. You cannot, he says, disown the authority by which alone you sit. There are some things which are *Fundamental*—guaranteed by the constitution and not to be altered by a vote of the House. These are: first, government by a Single Person and a Parliament, not by a particular person, but by a Single Person. "*In every Government there must be somewhat Fundamental, somewhat like a Magna Charta, which should be standing, be unalterable.*" Secondly, it is a Fundamental that Parliament should not make themselves perpetual. Thirdly, liberty of conscience in religion is a Fundamental. Fourthly, it is Fundamental that the military forces shall not be at the sole disposal either of Parliament or Executive, but held conjointly between them: not a man being raised, nor a penny charged on the People, nothing can be done without consent of Parliament; and in the intervals of Parliament, without consent of the Council. The Supreme Officer has thus a power co-ordinate with, and not dependent on, the Parliament. All other things, he says, are "Circumstantials"—to be regulated by Parliament—civil expenses, and ordinary legislation. On these things, cries the Protector, I am forced to insist. "Necessity hath no law." True, some men pretend necessities; but it would be

> mere pedantry, mere stupidity, to assert that there are no real necessities. "I have to say: the wilful throwing away of this Government, such as it is, so owned of God, so approved by men, so witnessed to. I can sooner be willing to be rolled into my grave and buried with infamy, than I can give my consent unto!"

Oliver's position was this. After twelve years of war and strife, the three nations were in a state of political, social, and religious chaos. The one power which maintained order was the regimented party, called the army. The army had formally called on its commander-in-chief to assume responsible government under a written constitution. He had done so: the whole magistracy and civil administration had accepted him; for many months had worked heartily in his service; the nation had ratified their choice. A House of Parliament had been summoned by his writs, on the authority of the new constitution. It was not for them to dispute or upset it. His own authority was prior, more truly national, and more really representative.

Members were called on to sign a declaration, "not to alter the government as settled in a Single Person and a Parliament." Some three hundred signed; the minority—about a fourth—refused and retired. Vane, Ludlow, Sidney, Marten, as consistent republicans, had even refused to be candidates. But neither Vane, Ludlow, nor Sidney were possible protectors of the Republic: and a Republic without a Head was an idle dream.

The Parliament, in spite of the declaration, set itself from the first to discuss the constitution, to punish heretics, suppress blasphemy, revise the Ordinances of the Council; and they deliberately withheld all supplies for the services and the government. At last they passed an Act for revising the constitution *de novo*. Not a single Bill had been sent up to the Protector for his assent. Oliver, as usual, acted at once. On the expiration of their five lunar months, 22nd January 1655, he summoned the House and dissolved it, with a speech full of reproaches. He said: "Dissettlement and division, discontent and dissatisfaction; together with real dangers to the whole,—have been more multiplied within these five months of your sitting than in some years before!" Then he enlarges on the dangers and confusions. A government, limited in a Single Person and a Parliament, had called them there as most agreeable to the general sense of the Nation, as most likely to avoid the extremes of Monarchy on the one hand, and of Democracy on the other;—and yet not to found Dominium in gratiû."

No Parliament was called for a year and eight months; the revival of insurrection drove Cromwell to attempt to govern by a system of provincial prefects, known as that of the major-generals; and the need of money forced him to a series of arbitrary methods for obtaining supplies. Both of these will be considered in the next chapter. It had been no part of Cromwell's scheme to suppress Parliaments. And he summoned another on 17th of September 1656. Immense efforts were made by the major-generals to exclude hostile candidates; and even after this, one hundred elected members were declared by the Council disqualified, and forcibly excluded from the House. Oliver addressed them in a long and memorable speech—partly a reasoned justification of his government; partly a magnificent Puritan sermon.

This Parliament was mainly occupied with a scheme for vesting the Crown in Oliver. The question of Cromwell assuming the monarchy, though intrinsically difficult to decide, is perfectly simple to follow. The majority in Parliament, the lawyers, the men of business, the more conservative of the Puritans, honestly desired it, as the only chance of an effective settlement. The nation was not actively averse. But the bulk of the army disliked it: most of the officers protested; the republicans, the Fifth Monarchy fanatics, the Bible zealots, were rabidly indignant. Cromwell himself was ready to take the title, if he could see "a clear call" to it. Now a "clear call" in his eyes was the preponderating voice of the religious, earnest, and thoughtful men of the party. That "call" he could not satisfy himself that he had received. And, deeply as his judgment assented to the reasons in its favour, he could not assume such an office, whilst it still was so wanting in the witnessing of conscience and of God.

The arguments that made for kingship were very real and very weighty. The office of King was known to the law, to the constitution, to the people. The prerogatives, rights, limits, and functions of the king were solidly settled by custom; bounded, said the lawyers, as well as any acre of land. Neither in law nor in public opinion was the throne destroyed when the king was dethroned. There stood the vacant place; which, in the minds of so many, Charles Stuart might any day return to fill. The institution itself was intact; and round it centred the law, the life of the body politic, the entire mechanism of administration. A "King" was a legal, constitutional, traditional, familiar functionary. A "Protector" was a provisional *locum tenens*, with no known prerogatives, no known limits, an indefinite and unfamiliar makeshift. The full force of this reasoning sank into Cromwell's brain. His sympathy with order, with established institutions, his yearning for a "settlement," his personal desire to legalise his own authority in the eyes of the entire nation—all pressed upon his judgment. Long he pondered, waited, compromised, sought for a witnessing from the Powers of Light and Truth. They still stood averse. He was now materially strong enough to have mastered opposition in the army. But morally, he could not so break with his own past, with his own spiritual life, with the godly men whom he had so long led, as to step into the seat of the king they had beheaded. Here, and for the last time, the army appears as the conscience of the nation. Steadily, and with dignity he put the Crown aside. He valued the title, he said, but "as a feather in his hat." If his judgment erred, his higher instinct was true. He never was greater than in refusing a dignity which would have taken all meaning out of the

Puritan Revolution—even though his refusal was certain to doom the Puritan Revolution itself as a premature and short-lived effort.

Though he refused the title of king, he accepted the new Protectorate on a revised basis, and was installed with the ceremonial of a coronation in Westminster Hall, 26th June 1657. Oliver had now the right of appointing his successor, and of creating a House of Lords. He was thus Sovereign in all but name: with ' something that could be called a national constitution and a Parliamentary title. The second protectorate Parliament on the Installation prorogued itself until January 1658. When it met on the second session, it was in a different temper. The excluded members were re-admitted: Haslerig, Scott, and the other malcontents were again the leaders of the House; and they at once began a deliberate campaign to destroy the constitution under which they met. Twice within five days the Protector poured out on them an impassioned discourse to consider the national perils, and to legislate instead of upsetting the established Government. He had taken his oath, he said, to govern according to the laws that were then made. "I sought not this place. I speak it before God, Angels, and Men: I did not. You sought me for it, you brought me to it; and I took my oath to be faithful to the interest of these nations, to be faithful to the Government." Parliament continued to assail the constitution. Ten days later the Protector suddenly dissolved them in a speech of burning indignation and proud defiance (4th February 1658).

> "There is not a man living can say I sought it (the place of Protector); no, not a man nor woman treading upon English ground. But contemplating the sad condition of these Nations, relieved from an intestine war into a six or seven years' Peace, I did think the Nation happy therein; I can say in the presence of God, in comparison with whom we are but like poor creeping ants upon the earth,—I would have been glad to have lived under my woodside,

> to have kept a flock of sheep—rather than undertake such a government as this. But undertaking it by the Advice and Petition of you, I did look that you who had offered it unto me should make it good." Then he dilates on the manifold perils to the State, within and without. "What is like to come upon this, the Enemy being ready to invade us, but even present blood and confusion? And if this be so, I do assign it to this cause: your not assenting to what you did invite me to by your Petition and Advice, as that which might prove the Settlement of the Nation. And if this be the end of your sitting, and this be your carriage—I think it high time that an end be put to your sitting. And I do dissolve this Parliament. And let God be judge between you and me."

Such was Oliver's last Parliament. His position now was the same as it was four years ago; the business of Parliament in the midst of a revolutionary crisis, at the close of a long civil war, was to pass laws and vote supplies, and not to reopen constitutional struggles. He never held another Parliament. His "Upper House," or "House of Lords," was an utter failure. He was planning the election of a third Parliament when his own end came.

Apart from opposition from his Parliaments, the Protectorate was one unbroken success. Order, trade, commerce, justice, learning, culture, rest, and public confidence, returned and grew ever stronger. Prosperity, wealth, harmony, were restored to the nation; and with these a self-respect, a spirit of hope and expansion such as it had not felt since the defeat of the Armada. Never in the history of England has a reorganisation of its administrative machinery been known at once so thorough and so sound. No royal government had ever annihilated insurrection and cabal with such uniform success, and with moderation so great. No government, not even that of Henry VII. or of Elizabeth, had ever been more frugal; though none with its resources had effected so much. No government had ever been so tolerant in things of the mind; none so just in its dealings with classes and interests; none so eager to suppress abuses, official tyranny, waste and speculation. No government had been so distinctly modern in its spirit; so penetrated with desire for reform, honesty, capacity. For the first time in England the republican sense of social duty to the State began to replace the old spirit of personal loyalty to a Sovereign. For the first and only time in modern Europe morality and religion became the sole qualifications insisted on by a Court. In the whole modern history of Europe, Oliver is the one ruler into whose presence no vicious man could ever come; whose service no vicious man might enter.

But it was in foreign policy that the immediate splendour of Oliver's rule dazzled his contemporaries. "His greatness at home," wrote Clarendon, "was but a shadow of the glory he had abroad." Englishmen and English historians have hardly even yet taken the full measure of the stunning impression produced on Europe by the power of the Protector. It was the epoch when supremacy at sea finally passed from the Dutch to the English. It was the beginning of the maritime Empire of England. And it was the first vision of a new force which was destined to exercise so great an influence, the increased power of fleets and marine artillery to destroy seaports and dominate a seaboard. Hitherto fleets had fought with fleets. But Blake taught modern Europe that henceforward fleets can control kingdoms. It was the sense of this new power, so rapid, so mobile, with so long an arm and practically ubiquitous, that caused Mazarin and Louis, Spain and Portugal, Pope and Princes of Italy, to bow to the summons of Oliver. England became a European Power of the first rank, as she never had been since the Plantagenets, not even in the proudest hours of Wolsey or Elizabeth. From the Baltic to the Mediterranean, from Algiers to Teneriffe, from Newfoundland to Jamaica, were heard the English cannon. And the sense of this new factor in the politics of the world produced on the minds of the age such an impression as the rise of the German Empire with the consolidation of the German military system has produced upon our own. All through his rule Oliver had laboured to found a vast Protestant League, a new Balance of Power. Had he ruled for another generation the history of Europe might have had some different cast.

It was not to be. The Protectorate fell in the zenith of its power: and there was silence on the earth for a space. For nearly two years more the Commonwealth held together: wholly without a Head, almost without a Government. Could it have been prolonged? Yes. Could it have been permanent? No. The Commonwealth and its government might well have lasted for the whole life of Oliver. But none, save he, could maintain it. And even he could not have made it lasting. The movement was essentially premature; not adequately prepared; from first to last the work of a minority, though a minority stronger, nobler, wiser than all the rest of the nation. Its dominant spirit, Puritanism, was fatally impracticable for constructive work as a political and social scheme. This the sublime common sense of Oliver forced upon him, step by step overpowering the intense devoutness of his faith. And ever larger as grew the statesman, less and less was Oliver the rigid Puritan, the literal Bible zealot.

Was then the work of his life a failure? Not so: for, in some sense, most of the great movements in history are for a time premature, and the labours of most great statesmen result in consequences that they little intend or conceive. How utterly does the history of England since 1640 differ from the history of England before that date!

Could Cromwell have maintained his system, had he lived? There is no reason to doubt it. No ruler in ancient or in modern times has ever surpassed him in the qualities of vigilance, caution, and foresight. As a statesman he happily rose superior to the chivalrous disregard of personal safety which had been fatal to Caesar, William the Silent, Henry

IV., and Buckingham. His almost miraculous insight into his enemies' plots and his sleepless watchfulness of public opinion give every ground for thinking that he would have been as successful in the future as he had been in the past. He may be said to be almost the one politician of the first rank continuously attended by uniform success: who had never been surprised by an enemy, and on whom no opponent had ever inflicted a disaster. The one condition of the maintenance of his rule was the duration of his life. Had his life been prolonged to the age of seventy-five—now almost the normal limit for modern statesmen—the Protectorate might have lasted for twenty years instead of five. It is perhaps not an idle dream that, in some way, it might have handed on a peaceful and reformed State to a constitutional Monarchy, without the debasing interlude of the Restoration. In 1674 William of Orange was twenty-four years of age, already a great captain and an experienced statesman, the hope of the Protestant cause and the bulwark in Europe against tyranny. Is it utterly impossible that the great Stadtholder might have peacefully succeeded the great Protector, under some national alliance, or even by the marriage of William with one of the family of Cromwell? England might have been spared the ignominy and the bloodshed of the restored Stuarts; the long English Revolution might have been a gradual and peaceful evolution from a feudal to an industrial, from a mediaeval to a modern polity; and the great Chief of the Commonwealth might have peacefully handed over a new and grander England to the great Founder of our Constitutional Monarchy.

CHAPTER XII

HOME POLICY OF THE PROTECTORATE

The internal policy of the Protector can only be understood if we regard him as a temporary Dictator set up to close an epoch of revolution and war. His rule was avowedly provisional and summary; based on expediency, necessity, and public peace. Constitutional right it could have none: it rested on the sword, as in times of revolution and civil war all government must rest. Cromwell's nature and genius were those of the practical man, dealing with the exigencies of the hour. He made no attempt to recast the political organism, or to found a brand-new set of institutions. As he said in Parliament, Healing and Settling were the crying needs of the time. He was the typical opportunist, doing what seemed best for the hour with the actual materials at hand. He did things quite as arbitrary as any Tudor or any Stuart. He did violent things—even odious things. He governed at times by sheer military force. But the true tests by which he must be judged are these. Was not his task essentially different from that of any Tudor, Stuart, or legitimate king? Was not his task an indispensable duty? Did he erect military government into a system, or carry arbitrary action beyond the immediate necessity? Was his government as a whole, given its revolutionary origin and its military basis, that of the self-seeking military tyrant? These questions each of us must answer according to his general view of this momentous epoch.

The first duty of the Protector was to keep order. He was the constable set to keep the peace in the parish. In a country torn by rebellion and war for fourteen years and on the verge of social dissolution, external order was the first pressing need. No English government had ever kept it better—not even that of Henry VIII. or Elizabeth at their best. Neither Wolsey, nor Thomas Cromwell, nor Burleigh, nor Walsingham, nor Salisbury, were more vigilant, better served with information, or more skilful in using it, than were Oliver and Thurloe. During the Commonwealth there was, we may say, one continuous plot to assassinate the Protector and to restore the Stuarts, starting with the infamous proclamation of Charles to reward Oliver's assassin. In these attempts Anabaptists, Fifth-Monarchy men, Republicans, Catholics, and Royalists were constantly conspiring. Each and all were easily and quietly crushed. Nor were they crushed with wholesale bloodshed. Some eight or ten distinct conspiracies are recorded, the authors of which were arrested upon clear evidence of designs to kill the Protector or to destroy his government. Many scores of conspirators were arrested. Four only were executed: Gerard, Vowel, Sir H. Slingsby, and Dr. Hewit. One plot only broke into an insurrection. In that, Penruddock and Grove, taken in arms, were beheaded; several other actual insurgents were hanged; many more transported to Barbadoes.

Penruddock's insurrection led to the very severe policy against the Royalists, by which they were amerced in the tenth of their fortunes. It was a crushing measure, but it can hardly be called vindictive or wanton. The system of Major-Generals by which it was carried out was an anticipation of the modern method of government by Prefects and Military Governors of provinces. Oliver called it his "little poor invention," and it was undoubtedly an engine of terrible power. It was in the highest degree arbitrary and without a shadow of legal right. It was, in fact, the military occupation of a country after insurrection, declared, as we now say, to be in a state of siege—a condition with which in modern Europe we are but too familiar, and one which no government can absolutely renounce. It was a war measure, to be justified only, if at all, by the exigencies of war. It lasted in vigour somewhat more than a year, and was a terror to the Royalists, but not to the public. Having served its turn, it was dropped, partly in consequence of the odium it caused, partly because it served as an expedient to undermine the Protector's authority.

Most of the eighty-two Ordinances passed by the Protector and his Council were subsequently confirmed by Parliament. They consisted of measures to continue Taxes and Excise, for reorganising the Church, reforming the law, for union of Scotland with England, for consolidating the Treasury, for the reform of colleges, schools, and charitable foundations, and for the suppression of cock-fighting, duelling, etc. etc. On the whole, this body of dictatorial legislation, abnormal in form as it is, in substance was a real, wise, and moderate set of reforms.

Taxation was throughout the great difficulty of the Protectorate, owing entirely to this: that Parliament so long occupied itself with checkmating or upsetting the Protectorate itself. This drove Oliver to measures which in point of constitutional law are quite as illegal as any device of James or Charles. And when he proceeded to procure the conviction of Cony, and actually sent to the Tower three eminent lawyers who claimed in his defence the ancient law of the land, it is open to any one to argue that this was as arbitrary as anything in the case of ship-money or the Impositions. The question for us is this: Was his arbitrary government in spirit and effect the same as that of Charles or James? As a matter of constitutional law the Protectorate as a whole is out of court altogether. Its sole plea is necessity. And though necessity is for the most part, as we know, the tyrant's plea, it is also at times the plea of the wise and just man in a great crisis.

If this arbitrary government had settled into a system, if it did not prepare for a return to a legal government by consent, Oliver stands condemned as a tyrant and not a Protector. It is possible that the situation was itself inherently impracticable, and the difficulties it presented may have been insuperable. But such as they were, each year of Oliver's short rule showed them as diminishing, and his power to control them as growing. The ancient organisation of England, political, judicial, administrative, ecclesiastical, and social—law, police, taxation, education, and government—had rested since the Conquest upon a king, a territorial Church, and a privileged territorial aristocracy. First the Church, and then the aristocracy, had broken away from the revolutionary movement and rallied round the king. Oliver found both fanatically hostile to Commonwealth and to himself. And he had to found order—parliamentary, judicial, administrative, and ecclesiastical—in a society where the old ministers of such order were bent on producing disorder. A permanent settlement was beyond the reach of human genius. Such temporary settlement as was possible Oliver made.

Apart from its dictatorial character, the Protector's government was efficient, just, moderate, and wise. Opposed as he was by lawyers, he made some of the best judges England ever had. Justice and law opened a new era. The services were raised to their highest efficiency. Trade and commerce revived under his fostering care. Education was reorganised; the Universities reformed; Durham founded. It is an opponent who says: "All England over, these were Halcyon days." Men of learning of all opinions were encouraged and befriended. "If there was a man in England," says Neal, "who excelled in any faculty or science, the Protector would find him out, and reward him according to his merit." It was the Protector's brother-in-law, Warden of Wadham College, who there gathered together the group which ultimately founded the Eoyal Society.

Noble were the efforts of the Protector to impress his own spirit of toleration on the intolerance of his age; and stoutly he contended with Parliaments and Council for Quakers, Jews, Anabaptists, Socinians, and even crazy blasphemers. He effectively protected the Quakers; he admitted the Jews after an expulsion of three centuries; and he satisfied Mazarin that he had given to Catholics all the protection that he dared. In his bearing towards his personal opponents, he was a model of magnanimity and self-control. Inexorable where public duty required punishment, neither desertion, treachery, obloquy, nor ingratitude ever could stir him to vindictive measures.

It is the high distinction of Oliver's Court that for once it exacted morality and purity from men as much as from women. He long refused his daughter's hand to the heir of the Earl of Warwick, because he was told the young man was given to play and other vices. The state kept by the Protector, though modest and serious, was neither gloomy nor uncouth. Oliver loved music, encouraged musicians, and held weekly concerts. He loved society; and was frank, humorous, and genial with his intimates; affable with dependants and strangers; stately and impressive on occasions of state. It is remembered to his honour that he preserved to our country the cartoons of Raffaelle, and the "Triumph" of Mantegna, together with some royal palaces and parks; that he collected a fine library; that he sought out and gathered round him many men of genius and learning. He was generous of his personal fortune, and made no use of power to extend it. He showed no disposition to nepotism; was exceedingly slow to advance his own sons; did nothing to promote the private interest of his own family. About his whole career there was no stain of personal interest. He made no serious attempt to found a dynasty. He made no definite nomination even of a successor. After his death, he knew too well, nothing which he could do would save the Cause. He accepted the inevitable—and he did nothing.

CHAPTER XIII

FOREIGN POLICY OF THE PROTECTORATE

Cromwell's foreign policy had one consistent aim: to form a great Protestant Alliance, and to place England at its head. It was a policy not of War, but of Defence; though peace was to be secured by the assertion of armed might on land and on sea. As a means to this end, it involved the destruction of the mercantile monopoly, first of the Dutch in Europe, and then of Spain in the west. In result, it placed England by one bound at the head of the powers of Europe; it laid the foundations of the naval supremacy of England, and also of her transmarine Empire; could it have been maintained unbroken down to the age of William III., it would have changed the whole history of Europe, and the latter half of the reign of Louis XIV. would have told a very different tale. Coming after the wars of religion, and before the dynastic wars and the commercial wars of the next hundred years, Cromwell's foreign policy was founded in part on religion, in part on trade. It was in no sense a policy of dynasty or of conquest. Had it been continued, it might have done much to prevent wars of dynasty and conquest. When the Commonwealth opened on the death of Charles I., England had sunk, both in credit and in power, to one of the lowest points known to her history. At the death of the Protector, she held a rank in the eyes of Europe such as she had never reached since the days of the Plantagenets, such as she has never reached since, but in the time of Marlborough, Nelson, and Wellington.

The war which finally wrenched from the Dutch the supremacy at sea was the work of the Commonwealth. In this Cromwell shared, but his part was not so great as that of Vane or Blake. But it was his privilege to tell his first Parliament, as Protector, that he had already made four honourable treaties of Peace. Within four months he made peace with Holland, with Sweden, with Denmark, with Portugal; and was negotiating peace with France. "Peace is desirable with all men," he said, "so far as it may be had with conscience and honour!" "There is not a nation in Europe but is very willing to ask a good understanding with you." It was a proud saying—and it was true.

Though he long made some politic hesitations, it is plain that, from the first, he honestly designed an alliance with France and not with Spain. And in this he was right, not only from the point of view of his time, but on a just estimate of the state of Europe. The safety of the Protestant cause was by no means yet secured; Spain, and not France, was then the head of the Catholic and retrograde forces; and the free commerce of the ocean was impossible whilst the exclusive pretensions of Spain existed. When Blake's guns destroyed fleet after fleet of Spain, when Penn and Venables conquered Jamaica, when Lockhart's red-coats swept away Don John's veterans, Cromwell was true to his idea of a great Protestant alliance, with England at its head.

All through his rule he laboured to unite the non-Catholic states—Sweden, Denmark, Holland, Brandenburg, and the other North German duchies, Switzerland, even Russia—"All the interests of the Protestants," he said, "are the same as yours"—regarding himself as the heir to the policy of Henry IV., of Elizabeth, of Gustavus Adolphus; preparing that of our own William of Orange. This policy reached its highest point in the magnificent burst of pity and indignation with which he championed the Vaudois against extermination: one of the noblest memories of England.

It is seldom that in the history of a country national pride and moral elevation surround the same deed. It is seldom that the foremost statesman of an age joins to himself the foremost poet of his time in expressing in one voice the religion, the sympathy, the power, the generosity of a great nation. "Avenge, O Lord, Thy slaughtered Saints," wrote Oliver's secretary in verse. "*Pulcherrimi facti laus atque gloria illibata atque integra tua erit*" he wrote in his Latin despatch from Oliver to Louis XIV. The sentence might serve for the Protector's epitaph.

The settlement of Scotland and its union with England was in every point of view one of the most complete of the Protector's works. Peace, order, justice, reform, prosperity, attended it in unbroken success. It is a Scotchman, and an opponent of Oliver, who has recorded, "We always reckon those eight years of the usurpation a time of great peace and prosperity." Far otherwise was it with Ireland. The conquest, begun by Oliver with ruthless cruelty, was completed by Ireton, Ludlow, and his other generals, with unflinching savagery. Famine, massacre, spoliation, transportation, persecution, and private murder, exterminated the Irish landowners in the larger part of the island. Wholesale dispossessions, proscriptions, and transplantation, transferred the bulk of the soil to Protestant adventurers. At length Ireland had peace; but it was the peace made by the destroyer, as of the Roman it was said, "They make a wilderness and call it peace." "No such doom," writes the historian of the English People, "had ever fallen on a nation in modern times as fell upon Ireland in its new settlement." And it was essentially the work of Oliver. For ten years, from 1649 to 1659, Ireland had no other rulers but Oliver, his two sons-in-law, his own son. In Scotland, religion, institutions, law, land, habits, and national sentiment were scrupulously respected. In Ireland, the religion, institutions, law, land, habits, and national sentiment of the Irish were trampled under the heel of the conqueror. Such is the dark side of Puritanism and of English ambition.

The same taint in a measure hangs over the war policy of Oliver in Europe, if we judge it by the standard of social morality and our modern desire for peace. In that age, and with such a creed, it would be asking too much to require such a standard of Puritans. Admitting its arrogant assertion of right and godliness, it was an unbroken and dazzling triumph. The history of England offers no such picture to national pride as when the kings and rulers of Europe courted, belauded, fawned on the farmer of Huntingdon. The record of English arms has no more brilliant page than that of Blake at Teneriffe, of Lockhart at Dunkirk and Morgan at Ypres, when the Ironsides stormed unbreached forts and annihilated Spanish battalions, to the amazement of Turenne, Conde, and Don John. Never has a ruler of England been formally addressed by kings in such Oriental terms as "the most invincible of sovereigns," "the greatest and happiest of princes." "It was hard to discover," wrote Clarendon, "which feared him most, France, Spain, or the Low Countries;" "There is nothing he could have demanded that either of them would have denied him." But, as in his own age, so perhaps still, the memory of Cromwell has impressed itself on the imagination of foreigners more deeply than on that of his countrymen. It is an eminent statesman and a great historian of another country who has written: "He is, perhaps, the only example which history affords of one man having governed the most opposite events, and proved sufficient for the most various destinies." It is a philosopher of another country who has said: "Cromwell, with his lofty character, is the most enlightened statesman who ever adorned the Protestant world."

CHAPTER XIV

THE LAST DAYS: SICKNESS AND DEATH

A.D. 1658. AETAT. 59

Never had the fortunes of the Cause stood firmer than in July 1658—had but Oliver been destined to live out his threescore years and ten. At home rebellion and plots had been once more utterly stamped out; abroad the capture of Dunkirk had raised the glory of England to its highest point; a new Parliament was preparing, it was hoped with happier prospects. But the wings of the Angel of Death already were hovering over the house of Oliver.

His youngest daughter Frances, a bride of three months, was made a widow in February, by the death of young Rich, grandson and heir to the Earl of Warwick. The old Earl, the staunchest friend of the Protector amongst the peers, followed his grandson in April. Next, in July, the Protector's favourite daughter, Elizabeth Claypole, lay dying at Hampton Court. She too had recently lost her youngest boy, Oliver. Now she was in great extremity of bodily pain, with frequent and violent convulsion fits. Through nearly all July the broken-hearted father hung over her bedside, unable to attend to any public business whatever. On 6th of August she was dead.

Oliver himself had sickened during her last days; and, though he came to London on the 10th, when she was buried in Henry VII.'s chapel, he returned to Hampton Court very ill. That day, it seems, in his bedchamber, he called for his Bible, and desired a godly person to read to him Philippians iv. 11, 12, 13; and repeating again and again the words: "*I can do all things through Christ that strengtheneth me*," he said thus to himself, "He that was Paul's Christ is my Christ too!" For some days longer he continued to transact business, and even took the air. There George Fox saw him for the last time. "As he rode at the head of his lifeguard, I saw and felt a waft of death go forth against him; and, when I came to him, he looked like a dead man."

The next day he was very ill with ague, which became "a bastard tertian," hot and cold shivering fits recurring at intervals. Between the attacks he did some business, and was able to be carried in a coach to Whitehall on the 24th. But "his time was come, and neither prayers nor tears could prevail with God to lengthen out his life." He saw Fairfax for the last time, and steadily refused his petition for the release of Fairfax's son-in-law, Villiers, Duke of Buckingham. He still in the intervals of the fever fits gave some orders, mitigated Buckingham's captivity, and made some appointments. But the ague became a "double tertian," fits recurring within the same day. "Truly the hot fit hath been very long and terrible," wrote Thurloe, "insomuch that the doctors fear he will scarce get through it." The family were all around him, except Henry, who was in Ireland. Hope was now given up; consternation fell on the household and the whole Puritan party; all through Sunday the churches resounded with prayers.

His faithful attendant has preserved a record of his last hours. These are some of his last words—but we must remember that, in such a malady, coherence is out of the question, even if deathbed speeches are ever exactly recorded. He spoke continually of the Covenants; the preachers, chaplains, and many others being constantly about him, or in the room adjoining. When his children and wife stood weeping round him, he said: "Love not this world. I say unto you, it is not good that you should love this world!" He prayed: "Lord, Thou knowest, if I do desire to live, it is to show forth Thy praise and declare Thy works!" Once he was heard saying, "It is a fearful thing to fall into the hands of the Living God." Again: "I think I am the poorest wretch that lives; but I love God; or rather, am beloved of God."

On Monday, 30th August, there raged a terrific storm, unroofing houses, uprooting trees, dealing desolation at sea. Superstition, party malice, made the most of this historic storm. The dying man was now conscious only partially and at intervals. They urged him to name his successor. The sealed paper with Richard's name in it could not be found. Was it Richard? No man now knows. Twice the sinking ruler is believed to have given some indistinct assent. These are the words which passed current as his last Prayer:

> "Lord, though I am a miserable and wretched creature, I am in covenant with Thee through grace. And I may, I will, come to Thee, for Thy people. Thou hadst made me, though very unworthy, a mean instrument to do them some good, and Thee service; and many of them have set too high a value upon me, though others wish and would be glad of my death; Lord, however Thou do dispose of me, continue and go on to do good for them. Give them consistency of judgment, one heart and mutual love; and go on to deliver them, and with the work of reformation; and make the Name of Christ glorious in the world. Teach those who look too much on Thy instruments, to depend more upon Thyself. Pardon such as desire to trample upon the dust of a poor worm, for they are Thy people too. And pardon the folly of this short Prayer:—even for Jesus Christ's sake. And give us a good night, if it be Thy pleasure. Amen."

These sentences are not given as the precise words he uttered, and, like all last prayers, they are manifestly arranged. Yet some such words he probably repeated after Dr. Owen, or Dr. Goodwin, at his side. They certainly present to us the spirit of his last thoughts.

For two or three days more, life still flickered; and we have a few broken sentences recorded, it seems quite literally, by his faithful attendant:

> "Truly God is good; indeed He is; He will not—" Then his speech failed him, but as I apprehended, it was, "He will not leave me." This saying "God is good," he frequently used all along; and would speak it with much cheerfulness, and fervour of spirit, in the midst of his pains. Again he said: "I would be willing to live to be further serviceable to God and His People; but my work is done. Yet God will be with His People."
>
> He was very restless most part of the night, speaking often to himself. And there being something to drink offered him, he was desired to take the same, and endeavour to sleep. Unto which he answered: "It is not my design to drink or sleep; but my design is, to make what haste I can to be gone."

Towards morning he used some expressions of consolation and peace, and some of deep humility and self-abasement. The day that dawned was his day of triumph, the 3rd of September, the day of Dunbar, and of Worcester. He was then speechless, and remained all day in a stupor; prayer, consternation, and grief, all around him. Between three and four in the afternoon the watchers by his bedside heard a deep sigh. Oliver was dead.

Appendix D

The vast issues which hung on the Protector's life and the unsolved question if he named a successor give more than usual interest to the character of his last illness. My friend, Dr. W. Howship Dickinson, of St. George's Hospital, has been so kind as to examine the recorded facts, and to send me a brief report. His opinion is, and Sir George Paget, Regius Professor of Physic at Cambridge, agrees, that

Oliver died essentially of ague, or some form of malarial fever, without any advanced organic disease such as would cause death; but of ague coming upon a man weakened by toil, anxiety, and gout. It is probable that, if Peruvian Bark, which was then more or less in use in England, had been administered in time, the Protector's life might have been extended. But there is reason to think that this remedy, about the time of Oliver's last illness, had fallen into temporary disrepute, in consequence of a death believed to have been caused by it. It might have subdued the ague; and there is no evidence of any other sufficient cause of death. In such a malady it is unlikely that, after 31st of August, any prolonged mental effort could have been made. One of his physicians told Sir P. Warwick that the Protector was "never in any such condition as distinctly to know what he did." And Dr. Bates declares that, when he is supposed to have nominated Richard, he was "in a drowsy fit."

His funeral was the most magnificent ever known in England. It was exactly imitated from that of Philip II., who had died on the same day, sixty years before, and is said to have cost in our values £150,000. The legends which have gathered round the remains of Oliver are almost as strange as those which are told of Alexander, Charlemagne, or Barbarossa. The ordinary histories record that the Protector's body was embalmed, buried in Henry VII.'s chapel, disinterred at the Restoration, hung at Tyburn, decapitated, and the head set up over the gate of Westminster Hall. It has been continually asserted (1) that his body was never buried in Westminster Abbey at all: (2) that it was buried on the field of Naseby; (3) that it was secretly sunk in the Thames; (4) that when disinterred at the Restoration, it was recovered by the family; (5) that, after hanging at Tyburn, it was buried near the foundations of No. 1 Connaught Place; (6) that it was obtained by Lady Fauconberg, and walled up in masonry at Newburgh in Yorkshire, which is still in the possession of Sir G. Wombwell, who inherits it from the

Fauconberg family. The truth it is now perhaps impossible to recover. The whole funeral ceremony was avowedly performed with an "effigy." The more probable account would be, that the body was really buried in the Abbey, and was disinterred at the Restoration, and the head was actually exposed for many years over Westminster Hall. It is far from improbable that Lord Fauconberg had influence enough to secure the remains, and privately immured them in the walls of the mansion, where so many relics of Oliver remain.

If this be so, the quickened conscience of the nation might yet reverse a deed which dishonours our Monarchy and stains our annals; and the bones of the greatest ruler this country ever had might again be laid to rest beside the heroes and statesmen of England.

Printed in Great Britain
by Amazon

48536445R00116